501
SEWING HINTS

from the viewers of **sewing with nancy**®

Oxmoor
House®

501 SEWING HINTS
from the viewers of Sewing With Nancy®
from the "Sewing With Nancy" series

© 1995 by Oxmoor House, Inc.
Book Division of Southern Progress Corporation
P.O. Box 2463, Birmingham, Alabama 35201
Published by Oxmoor House, Inc., and Leisure Arts, Inc.

Library of Congress Catalog Number: 95-71254
Hardcover ISBN: 0-8487-1451-2
Softcover ISBN: 0-8487-1464-4
Manufactured in the United States of America
Second Printing 1996

Editor-in-Chief: Nancy Fitzpatrick Wyatt
Senior Crafts Editor: Susan Ramey Cleveland
Senior Editor, Editorial Services: Olivia Kindig Wells
Art Director: James Boone

501 SEWING HINTS

Editors: Lois Martin, Linda Baltzell Wright
Editorial Assistant: Catherine Barnhart Pewitt
Copy Editor: L. Amanda Owens
Designer: Emily Albright Parrish
Production and Distribution Director: Phillip Lee
Associate Production Manager: Theresa L. Beste
Production Assistant: Marianne Jordan Wilson
Senior Photographer: John O'Hagan
Photographers: Ralph Anderson, Keith Harrelson
Photo Stylist: Katie Stoddard

Editorial Assistance, Nancy's Notions: Susan Roemer
Illustrators: Rochelle Stibb, Cyd Moore

Dear Sewing Friends!

I love hints! I seek tidbits of information from wise friends and relatives when it comes to treating a bee sting, prompting my cactus to bloom, or keeping my husband and me on speaking terms when wallpapering! When it comes to sewing hints, my field of experts includes the knowledgeable sewing enthusiasts who watch my TV program, "Sewing With Nancy."

Each week on "Sewing With Nancy," I share five or six hints from my viewers. After nine years of collecting hints, we culled many of my favorite ideas and created *501 Sewing Hints*. I know you'll continually refer to different sections of this book and pick up new information each time.

So, why wait any longer! There are 501 hints just waiting to be tried!

Nancy Zieman

P. S. We receive hundreds of hints each month, including duplicate ideas. Since it is impossible to mention all people who send in the same idea, we've given credit to the first person or persons to send in the hint.

C O N T

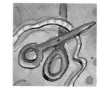

E N T S

BASIC SEWING TECHNIQUES 71

EMBELLISHMENTS 95

SPECIALIZED SEWING 115

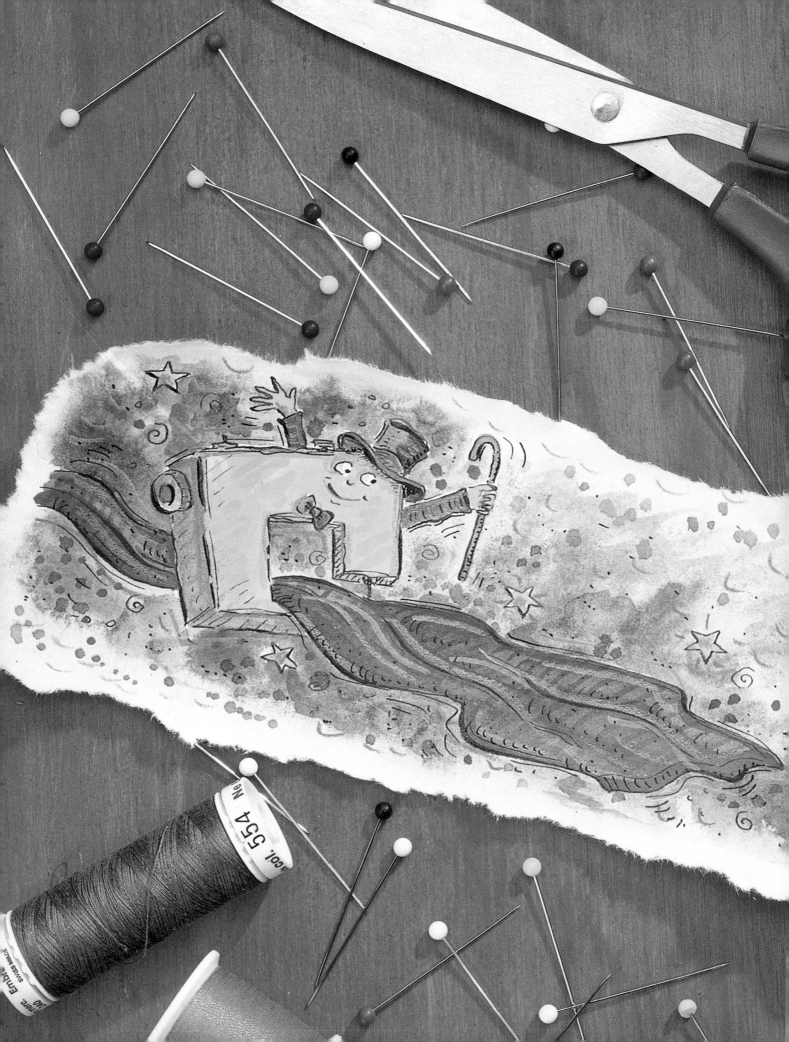

ORGANIZING

The ideal sewing room would have plenty of storage space, the latest equipment, and a simple system to keep all those sewing tools and notions right at your fingertips.

Few of us have ideal places in which to sew—we live in small houses or apartments, or we never seem to find the time to organize everything just the way we'd like. Not to worry. Here you'll find lots of helpful (and inexpensive) ways to arrange your sewing space so that you can save time and money and get more professional results.

Whether you're setting up equipment, doing the laundry, or trying to find places to store everything from patterns to sequins, "Sewing With Nancy" viewers have lots of commonsense ideas to help.

EQUIPMENT

Start with the basics—your sewing machine and serger, a cutting table, scissors, and some safety tips.

Sewing Corner

Turn even a small corner into a sewing center: I bought an inexpensive (under $100) computer table for my sewing machine. It included a typing table extension for my serger. I put the two tables at right angles with my ironing board behind, creating a U shape.

Susan Clark, Channahon, IL

Sewing Corner

Portable Sewing

I put casters on the legs of my sewing machine cabinet and attached a clamp lamp to the machine. Then I plugged the lamp and the machine into an extension cord with a triple outlet on the end. Now I can roll my machine to different parts of the house and sew while cooking a pot of soup, doing laundry, monitoring the backyard through a window, or watching TV. *Carol Childress, Roanoke, VA*

Dancing Machines

To keep my serger and sewing machine from walking as I sew, I place a carpet sample under each. Not only do the carpet samples keep the machines from walking or jiggling, they also catch a lot of threads and scraps that would otherwise fall onto the floor. (Clean threads from the carpet with a piece of masking tape.) *Lee Gaber, Issaquah, WA and Sue Wyszynski, Vancouver, WA*

Other ideas: *Diane Piergallini of Phoenix, AZ,* puts bubble packing material, bubble side down, between the machine and the table. *Lisa Bendler of Wauwatosa, WI,* puts a rubber car mat under her serger. To keep the machine foot pedals from slipping, *Josephine Reid of Metairie, LA,* glues a strip of nonskid fabric to the bottom of each pedal.

Serger Reference Cards

I have owned a serger for seven years but recently bought a new one. I have since spent many hours playing with different techniques. A minor change in needle tension, stitch length, thread, or fabric can make great differences in the finished effect.

I log tension and other settings, thread, and fabric on a note card. Then I glue a fabric sample stitched with those settings and thread onto the card. The next time I want a certain look, I just go through my samples, thus saving time by not having to re-create an effect. *Dottie Stelmacher, Fond du Lac, WI*

Note from Nancy

An easy way to record those settings is to fill out Serger Reference Cards. These 3" x 5" (7.5-cm x 12.5-cm) index cards have space for writing down the settings and any special techniques, plus room for attaching a fabric scrap with the completed stitching. Store the cards in a recipe file or a small box. The same system works for recording stitch samples for a sewing machine.

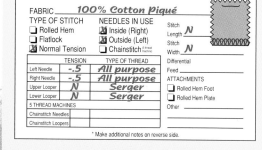

Serger Reference Card

Maximum Surge Protection

A sewing teacher warned us that a surge protector outlet strip must be on at all times to protect the machines. Now I leave my strip on but make sure that when I leave my sewing room, my machines are turned off. I use a separate outlet for my iron that I cannot miss seeing when I leave the room so that I'm sure it's unplugged.

Betty Kadeg, Seattle, WA

Note from Nancy

Some surge protector strips are designed to be left on at all times and others can be turned off when you leave the room. Check the box your surge protector came in (or look at any accompanying instruction sheets) to be sure of proper use for your surge protector.

Magnifying Safety

Be certain your glass magnifying lamp is covered when not in use. Sunlight streaming through the glass can quickly start a flame. I learned this by experience when I found my sewing cabinet smoking. Fortunately, I discovered the problem before the cabinet actually caught on fire, but I do have quite a noticeable burn mark.

Joan Engelbrecht, Bethlehem, PA

Tension

My sister and a friend were having problems figuring out which thread tension needed to be adjusted on their sergers. For each machine, I changed the threads to four different colors. I serged a test sample on a fabric scrap and then adjusted one tension at a time, serging another sample after each to check the adjustment. When all adjustments were made, I rethreaded each machine with one color thread and serged another sample to see if there were any other problems.

Jerrie Fry, Yuba City, CA

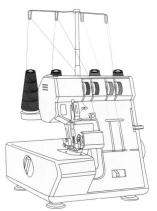

Colored Serger Threads

Machine Cover-up

I've found a quick, inexpensive way to make a sewing machine cover. I took a pretty pillowcase, cut it off at the correct height, made square corners, and stitched it. It's the perfect size for a machine and is very attractive.

Betty Rowe, Baytown, TX

A Sewing Machine Home

We got tired of seeing my sewing machine on the dining room table, so I enlisted my husband's creative talents to design a unique cover. Now the first thing you see when you come into our house is "our house."

I measured my machine and drew a pattern following the basic design of our home. I used quilted fabric remnants to stitch the house and the roof. Then I zigzagged windows to simulate our real ones and added ¾" (1.8-cm) black bias tape shutters and an appliquéd front door.
Elizabeth Fromm,
Royal Oak, MI

CLEANING AND MENDING

Save time cleaning (including laundry) and mending, and you'll have more time to sew!

Three Steps to Completion

Too much purchased fabric never becomes finished products. Increase your completion percentage by understanding the three basic parts of any project: First, get organized. Be sure you have all the tools and materials ready. Second, tidy up. As the sewing progresses, occasionally straighten up your work area so that it continues to be orderly. Third, and most important, when your sewing project is finished, put things away. Without this final step, the job never seems quite done.
Carol Tyler, Davis, CA

Velcro Thread Catcher

To prevent the mess of clipped threads on the floor, I attached a 5" (12.5-cm) strip of Velcro (the hook side) to the flatbed of my sewing machine using double-sided tape. As I clip, I pass the thread over the Velcro, which grabs and holds it securely, and I clean the strip after each project.
Baben Patricelli, Boone, NC

Blow-dried Sergers

I use a blow-dryer to clean my serger between projects. It quickly flushes out lint and scraps. I use an accessory brush to get to any nooks and crannies that the dryer misses. Now I can get ready for my next garment in record time!
Sue Bassiri, Beaverton, OR

Note from Nancy

To instantly remove lint and dust, you can also use a mini vacuum kit that attaches to the hose of your vacuum cleaner. Also use it to clean your VCR, computer keyboard, and camera!

A Jewel of a Bobbin

After moving to Florida from Massachusetts, I noticed signs of corrosion on my metal bobbins, perhaps due to the higher humidity. I cleaned the bobbins by immersing them in liquid jewelry cleaner for two hours. They came out almost like new.
Helen McCormack, Sun City Center, FL

Serger Catchall

After I used my serger several times, I found my floor (as well as myself) covered with fuzz and small fabric strips. I took a sandwich-sized zip-top plastic bag, cut it open at the bottom, and cut about 1" (2.5 cm) on each side. Then I folded down one cut edge and taped it in place. I also taped about 1" (2.5 cm) up each side of the bag so that the edges of the bag are stiff. I attached the remaining cut edge of the bag to my machine with more tape.

Now I brush fuzz and clippings into the bag as I serge. When the bag is full, I hold a trash can under it, unzip the bottom of the bag, and all the trimmings fall out without any mess on the floor or on me. I roll the bag up close to the machine when it's not in use.
Georgiana Carlisle, Laveen, AZ

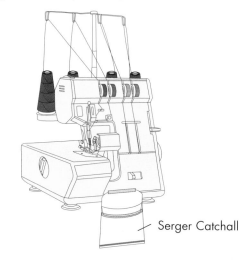

Serger Catchall

Note from Nancy

Several people sent in similar hints to Georgiana Carlisle's. I hope all you serger owners will take advantage of this handy device!

Vacuumless Thread Pickup

I use a sticky tape-backed (lint) roller to pick up threads that fall onto the carpet. It saves me from having to drag out the vacuum every time I finish sewing.
Terry Swanson, Honolulu, HI

De-Fusing Fabric

If I goof and get fusible web somewhere it doesn't belong, I use adhesive remover, which is sold at medical/surgical supply stores. With a cotton ball, I rub the remover into the unwanted web; then I wait a few minutes and rub some more. It may take several applications, but the web will come off. Of course, I try the remover on a scrap of the fabric before using it on a garment.
Donna Todd, Swartz Creek, MI

Preventing Problems

I sew a lot of appliqués and use fusible interfacing to give the fabrics support. I place an old pillowcase over the end of my ironing board to prevent fusible material from getting on my ironing board cover. The pillowcase works great and is so much easier to clean than the ironing board cover.
Phyllis Willis, Long Beach, CA

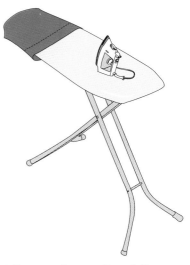

Pillowcase Ironing Board Cover

Deep Cleaning

To remove mineral deposits from inside an iron, I fill the iron with equal parts of distilled water and white vinegar, letting the iron steam for several minutes before unplugging it. I let it stand for an hour, empty the iron, and rinse with clear water.
Joanne Rock, Covington, VA

Cleaning Fusible Web from Irons

I keep a 12" (30-cm) square of netting on hand in case I get fusible interfacing on the bottom of my iron. I warm the iron, wad the netting into a ball, and gently rub the iron with the netting. The netting won't scratch the surface, yet it quickly removes the adhesive.
Marjorie Latimer, Burlington, Ont., Canada
Other ideas: *Anita Klatkiewicz of Sheboygan Falls, WI,* folds a brown grocery sack over the edge of her ironing board; while the iron is hot, she rubs it over the edge until the adhesive comes off on the paper. *Patricia Rosenthal of Random Lake, WI,* sprays WD-40 penetrating oil on her iron and then wipes off the adhesive and the oil.

> **Note from Nancy**
> Since WD-40 has a strong odor, I recommend using it outside whenever possible.

Laundry Care Labels

I sew long-distance for my daughter-in-law, and she needs to know the fiber content and care instructions for the garments. Rather than sending a separate note with that information, I sew the instructions onto the hem or neck facing of the garment using the alphanumeric symbols on my computerized sewing machine. This works out very well for us. It's also fun to include messages such as "Happy Birthday."
Ann Gamble, Onalaska, WI

Safety Tip

Be very careful with clear thread scraps. Pets have been hurt by eating them. Barbara Meyers, Bolingbrook, IL

Spot Cover-up

I stained the top to a new solid-colored interlock pant set and could not remove the spot. I couldn't wear it as it was, so I figured I had nothing to lose by modifying it. Over the stained area, I appliquéd flowers cut from a floral print knit fabric and added little beads to the centers of the flowers. I also made matching pants from the floral fabric, so now I have both plain and floral pants to wear with the top. Noreen Falkner, Dunsford, Ont., Canada

Inflated Sleeves

When mending sleeves or pant legs, I roll up a magazine, insert it into the sleeve or pant leg, and let the magazine fan open. This inflates the area needing work, making it easier to see and to mend.
Pat Osgerby,
Euless, TX

Save on Dry Cleaning

To save on dry-cleaning costs, I temporarily insert dress shields into the armholes of my suits and blouses. I apply a temporary fabric glue at both ends of the shield and then stick the shield to the garment or the lining. The shields are easy to remove and reuse in other garments. I clean the shields after each wearing and dry-clean the garment as needed.
Sally Emerson,
Stoddard, WI

French Knots Code Laundry

To eliminate washday problems, I color-code my latest creations with colored French knots so that I can remember at a glance how to launder the garments. It saves the time required to sew in a care label, which may fade and scratch against tender skin. The coding I use is as follows:

Water Temperature		Drying	
Hot	●	Line dry	● ●
Cold	●	Dryer	●
Warm	●		

Laurie Kirchhoff, New Baltimore, MI

French Knot Color Coding

Kids Clothing Labels

I make 90% of my four children's clothes and try to coordinate the fabrics that I use. To help all the children get dressed, I sew ¼" x 1" (6-mm x 2.5-cm) swatches of fabric into the garments that match the swatch fabric. First I apply a heavy fusible interfacing to a swatch and sometimes zigzag the edges to prevent raveling. I then stitch the swatch into the waistband or a seam of the garment. On busy school mornings, this saves much time and frustration, since each child can choose a coordinated outfit by selecting pieces that have the same fabric swatches.
Jennifer Jarrett, Copperas Cove, TX

Roses to Go

I have a white top that is embellished with fabric roses and bows. The care label indicates that the top is washable, but I don't feel that the roses and the bows are. I removed them and then reattached them with snaps. Now when I launder the top, all I have to do is unsnap the roses and the bows and throw the top in the wash.
Olga Mary Quattrocchi, Tallmadge, OH

Note from Nancy

You can also use Velcro to attach embellishments. This hint works for any item with added embellishments, such as guest towels or decorative pillow covers.

Cleaning Blood from Fabric

To remove blood from a sewing project, I use a cotton ball and hydrogen peroxide immediately. The blood comes right out.
Geraltine Knight, Moultrie, GA

Washing Pillows

For years I have been frustrated by fiberfill that shifts when I wash and dry bed pillows. I finally hit on using a quilting technique. Before washing the pillows, I use a large darning needle and doubled thread to tie knots through the fiberfill, just like when I tie a quilt. The fiberfill stays in place beautifully. After the pillows dry, I remove the ties.
Jan Kosower, Eau Claire, WI

Staystitch Before Prewashing

In the past when I prewashed new fabric, the cut edges often frayed quite a bit and sometimes the frayed threads would get entangled with other items being washed. Now I use the overlock stitch of my serger (or my sewing machine's zigzag stitch) on the cut edges before prewashing. This solves two problems: fabric doesn't fray when prewashed, and I know which fabrics have been prewashed just by looking at the cut edges.
Vivian Janes, Hixton, WI

Handy Needles

I keep a thick pot holder on the wall near my washing machine. I put sewing needles threaded with basic colors in the pot holder, ready to sew on those buttons that sometimes come off in the washing machine or the dryer.
Annetta Dunlap, Grove City, PA

Branding T-shirts

Recently my 11-year-old son came home from school with a hole in one of his good T-shirts. I tried mending it, but it just didn't look good. The tear was at the bottom of the shirt, so I removed the brand-name label from the inside (at the back neck) and trimmed the part that states the size. I applied the label to the hole with a fusible adhesive and zigzagged around the edges. It looks very nice, and I doubt if anyone will ever know it didn't come that way.
Beth Machen, Pleasanton, TX

Socks Replace Worn Pajama Feet

Most of my oldest child's clothes last long enough to be handed down to my two younger children—except for the plastic soles on sleepers. I tried cutting off the soles and putting socks on the children, but the sleeper legs crawled, and the kids slipped because the socks didn't have a nonskid surface. So I purchased nonslip-soled socks and sewed one sock to the bottom of each leg of the worn sleepers.
Penny Williams, Portage La Prairie, Man., Canada

Pockets Everywhere

With four boys, I've learned to recycle jeans. My boys haven't been too fond of patches until I thought of using pockets for patches. I save the pockets from old jeans and jean jackets that are no longer wearable. When I need a patch, I take a pocket and serge around the edges, with fusible thread in the lower looper. Then, using fusible web the size of the pocket, I double-fuse the pocket into place. My guys love all the extra pockets that don't look like patches.
Media Witten, Virginia Beach, VA

No-Sew Patches

My husband wanted a number of patches put on a shirt to wear the next day. Because I'm quite slow at hand sewing, I was quick to think of an easier way to accomplish this task. I used LiquiFuse on the backs of the patches, but because the fronts have thick designs, I was concerned about ironing from the front. I used Sewer's Fix-It Tape on the front of the shirt to hold the patches in place and then lightly fused from the wrong side of the shirt. I removed the tape to prevent any sticky residue and then continued pressing from the inside until I got a good bond. It's been through the washer and the dryer many times and still holds tight.
Lila Young, Hamilton, MI

Note from Nancy

LiquiFuse is comparable to fusible web in a bottle. Apply it like glue and dry with a hair dryer. After positioning the trim, press with an iron. LiquiFuse permanently bonds layers together after heat-setting but is removable if washed out before it's ironed.

Pajama Patches

I found that iron-on stabilizing tricot makes very satisfactory patches for pajama elbows and other lingerie and sleepwear. Two scraps of the tricot, facing each other and sandwiching the weak spot in the fabric, can be quickly ironed in place, creating a patch that is just as soft and comfortable as the garment itself.
Anita Owen, North Plainfield, NJ

Attracting Pins

When cleaning up after sewing, I use a small magnet glued to the end of a yardstick to easily pick up pins and needles.
Ethel Barsness, Starbuck, MN

Quick Reminder

My husband sometimes asks me to mend a shirt with a loose pocket or a missing button, or a pair of pants with a zipper pulling out or a hole in the pocket. In the past, I often couldn't remember what he had asked me to do by the time I finally got to my sewing table to do the repairs. Now when he brings me some mending, I jot down the problem on a Post-it Note and stitch or pin the note to the garment so that when I sit down to mend, I can tell right away what needs to be repaired.
Mary Gemski,
Hampton, VA

Keep a misting bottle near your dryer to spray water on clothes that are wrinkled as they come out of the dryer. Just put the clothes on hangers, mist, and shake. Most wrinkles will fall right out. Hang up the clothes in a well-ventilated area and let them dry thoroughly.
Annetta Dunlap,
Grove City, PA

New Life for Sweatpants

I was about to cut off my younger son's favorite sweatpants to make shorts when I found that only the knee areas were worn. So I revamped the pants, adding length to accommodate his growth. After cutting out the worn knee sections, I cut doubled strips of contrasting sweatshirt fabric to add cushioning, each equal to the width of a removed knee section plus seam allowances and the amount my son had grown since the pants were new. After I sewed the contrasting fabric in place, the pants were as good as new. To my son, they were better than new—he loved the red knees on his favorite royal blue pants and wore them often until the entire garment wore out!
Dianne Leber, Kent, WA

Contrasting Patches

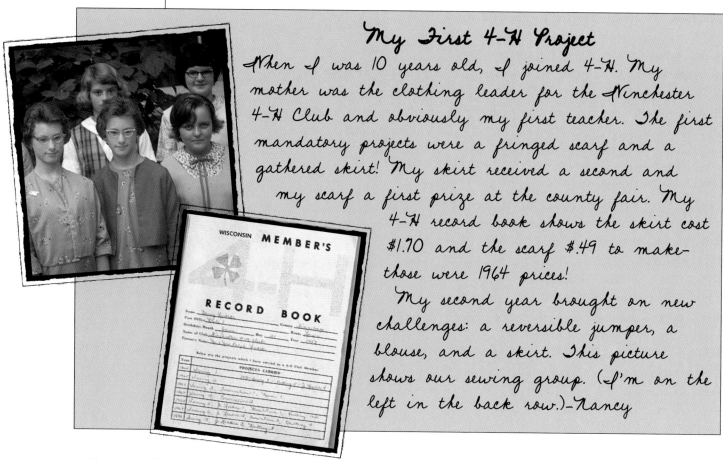

My First 4-H Project

When I was 10 years old, I joined 4-H. My mother was the clothing leader for the Winchester 4-H Club and obviously my first teacher. The first mandatory projects were a fringed scarf and a gathered skirt! My skirt received a second and my scarf a first prize at the county fair. My 4-H record book shows the skirt cost $1.70 and the scarf $.49 to make—those were 1964 prices!

My second year brought on new challenges: a reversible jumper, a blouse, and a skirt. This picture shows our sewing group. (I'm on the left in the back row.)–Nancy

FABRIC AND PATTERN STORAGE

Almost anyone who sews seems to become a "fabricaholic"—one who is addicted to collecting fabric. Finding a way to store all that fabric (and the patterns) can become a lifetime quest.

Computerized Fabric Inventory

As a fabricaholic, I find it much easier to buy fabric than to sew it. I use the data base management program on my home computer to keep track of all the fabric I have on hand. The fields in the data base allow me to record each type of fabric, the fiber content, the color(s), the care instructions, the amount, the width, the planned use, the season, the price per yard, the total price, and any notes or comments.

I keep a current printout pinned to the wall in my sewing room. Realizing how many entries are on the list also helps me resist the temptation to buy more!
Linda Boelter, Rhinelander, WI

Other viewers suggest: *Etta Katsma of Randolph, WI*, washes and remeasures all new fabric and then labels it, including what she paid for the fabric; that helps her keep track of the cost of projects. *Edith Agard of St. Germain, WI*, uses an extra closet or a clothes pole mounted in a corner to hold her fabric stash. She folds and hangs the yardage on hangers and puts a tag over the hook of each hanger with yardage and fiber content information. Clear plastic sweater files (a type of garment bag) let *Pat Bartels of Appleton, WI*, keep her fabric dust free but visible, with yardage and other information on cards pinned to fabric.

Prewash Lace

I buy laces and trims in large yardages and then prewash and dry each length in a mesh bag as I would after a delicate garment is finished. The mesh bag keeps the lace or the trim from getting all wound up and tied into knots. By prelaundering, my finished project looks much nicer because there's no shrinkage.
Roberta Mosher, Canon City, CO

Open a Fabric "Store"

I stock a steel shelving unit with fabric according to types and uses: girls' tops, suits, dresses, blouses, pajamas, men's shirts, etc. When someone needs a new garment, we simply look at the appropriate stack to make a selection. I stock the shelves with bargain purchases so that my children can "shop" without being tempted by expensive fabrics in a store. I also change the selection with the season— for example, in the spring, fleece and wool go into storage and out come cotton prints.
Sally Emerson, Stoddard, WI

Metal Shelving

Hanging Patterns

After I cut out a pattern and iron the pattern pieces, I hang the pieces from a plastic slacks hanger, pinning small pieces to larger ones. This is particularly helpful when I plan to reuse a pattern soon, since I don't have to fold it to store it and later reiron it. I also hang pattern pieces as I remove them from my current project so that they don't pile up or float around. They're also readily available for me to use to check a marking or a button spacing.
Bunny Schmidt, San Diego, CA

Recycle Patterns

Before discarding patterns, save the pieces that you like for collars, sleeves, and pockets. When you want to change a pattern, you'll have a stock of alternatives on hand for the alteration.
Joy Sexton,
Wanatah, IN

For patterns that include two or three garments (such as a jacket, pants, and a skirt), I use colored dots to identify each unit. I use red dots on each jacket pattern piece, blue on pant pieces, yellow on skirt pieces, and so on. I use the same colored dots to identify the garments on the front of the envelope. I can find the right pattern pieces quickly, simply by flipping through the dotted pieces.
Silvia Sisneros,
Dallas, TX

Pattern Folders

I used to have a hard time fitting all the pattern pieces back into the pattern envelope. Now I recycle a manila folder by machine-stitching the sides closed to form a roomy pocket in which to put pattern pieces. Then I slit the pattern envelope open along one side and the bottom so that it spreads out flat and glue or tape the envelope to the front of the folder. Folders such as this store neatly in a standard file cabinet, and each folder has plenty of room to hold fabric swatches from garments made using its pattern.
Jane Easton, West Union, IA

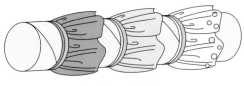

Pattern Folder

Store Trims on Baby Hangers

I keep elastics, laces, and trims wrapped around baby clothes hangers (the square ones that no one else knows what to do with). You can hang them up or store them flat, which-ever is more convenient.
Phyllis Kinneman, Hager City, WI

Baby Clothes Hanger

Tubes for Lace and Trims

I save the cardboard tubes from aluminum foil, paper towels, toilet tissue, wrapping paper, etc., and wrap onto them laces, trims, ribbons, and fabrics that should not be folded or creased. A rubber band holds each article tightly on the tube. (Pins rust in high humid-ity, leaving stains.) These tubes are abundant and can be cut to the exact size needed and then discarded when no longer useful.
Mary Black, Ava, MO

Cardboard Tube

Another idea: For small trims such as ribbon, *Paula Dyer of Hohenwald, TN,* uses empty thread spools or cones, taping one end of ribbon to the spool, winding the ribbon around, and securing the other end with a pin or a rubber band. Store the spools on a Peg-Board.

STORING NOTIONS

Where can you put thread and buttons and needles and pins and all those other small items that are essential to sewing? Read on as viewers share ways that they organize their sewing rooms.

Canned Thread

When I finish sewing a project, I like to keep my bobbin with the corresponding spool of thread. I cut a soda straw a little longer than the combined length of the spool and the bobbin and then I insert the straw into the bobbin and down through the spool. I keep the bobbin/spool combinations in round tins, such as those cookies or fruitcakes come in, storing different color tones in different cans (reds and pinks in one, blues in another, etc.). *Mary Duckworth, Cottonwood, AZ*

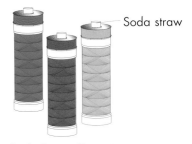

Soda straw

Soda Straw Organizer

Thread in Freezer Bags

I do machine embroidery and have many spools of rayon thread. I sew gallon freezer bags to fit the spools. I can easily see my colors, and the spools are neat and out of the dust.
Frances Mattson, Buena Park, CA

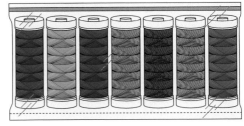

Freezer Bag

Spicy Thread

I had often been frustrated by having to dig through a drawer for a specific color spool of thread. Then, as I was sorting through some household items, I discovered a spice rack from my kitchen that I wasn't using. I hung it on the wall next to my sewing machine and put the spools of thread on it.
Earlean Wagner, Norwalk, CA

Thread Peg-Board

On two walls in my sewing room, within easy access of my sewing machine, I have spools of thread arranged in rows according to color hanging on Peg-Board. After many years of sewing, I've accumulated a large number of old spools. To keep track of what's old and what's new at a glance, I use a permanent marker to jot the month and the year of purchase at one end of each spool. Then when I'm clean-finishing cut edges of new fabrics before sewing, I reach up and choose any outdated spool.
Bonnie Lapka, O'Fallon, IL

Colored Threads

Timesaving Notion

To save an extra half hour to one hour every day for sewing, remember your freezer! When you cook, cook for an army. It usually doesn't take any longer to cook for a large group than for your family. Package and freeze the excess, and after a bit of stockpiling, you have meals that only require heating up in the oven— while you sew, sew, sew!
Barbara Esquivel,
San Diego, CA

Recycle Fusible Scraps

Whenever I patched elbows or knees, no matter how I pinned, the patch would slip a bit and not end up smooth or exactly where I wanted it. Now I use several small scraps of fusible web to fuse the patch before sewing, and I have neat patches in the correct places.
Ann Kempen, Kaukauna, WI

Cones on Slacks Racks

As a space-saver and organizer in my sewing room, I put cone thread on slacks racks and hang the racks in the closet. I am able to get three or more cones on each level, so I fit at least 12 cones per rack. The thread is easy to see and remove. Best of all, this organizer costs less than $5 per rack!
Jean McGuire, New Berlin, WI

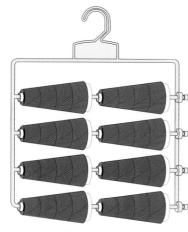

Slacks Hanger

Shoe Bag for Cones

I enjoy being able to find sewing supplies in a hurry. I've found that a hanging shoe organizer with clear pockets holds lots of cone thread and easily shows the colors. I hang the organizer on the wall behind my sewing room door.
Ida Fellers, Alamogordo, NM

Another idea: When *Audrey Dubois of Sun Lakes, AZ,* goes south for the winter, she takes all her sewing supplies in a clear plastic shoe organizer. She notes that the bag lies flat in a suitcase for traveling, and the sturdy hanger at the top lets her hang the bag in clear view in her sewing room. She suggests using a shoe organizer for notions and other sewing supplies in a dorm room, a small apartment, or any place where portability is a major concern.

Cone Thread Covers

I roll pieces of paper 2¾" x 7" (6.8 cm x 17.5 cm) into tubes and use them to cover my woolly nylon and metallic thread cones. I make a small cut at the bottom of each tube and insert the thread tail. This keeps the tails handy and the thread neat and clean.
Charlee Tumbleson, St. Petersburg, FL

Cone Thread Covers

Another idea: *Mary Yothers of Greensburg, PA,* makes cone thread sleeves from leftover pantyhose simply by cutting tubes the right length and stretching the sleeves over the cones.

Note from Nancy
Woolly nylon and metallic threads attract lint and dust, so thread cone covers help keep these kinds of thread clean and ready to use.

Interfacing Envelope

I make a storage envelope for interfacing out of the plastic interleaf (which has the instructions) included when you buy interfacing. I use a piece of the interleaf that is long enough to include two sets of instructions plus a flap. I fold the instruction sheet at the bottom of the first set of instructions and sew the sides together. I store each type of interfacing in its own envelope. Since the interleaf gives complete instructions for using the interfacing, I have no more questions about the weight and the bias or how to apply it. The envelope also keeps the interfacing clean and small pieces together.
Esther Shafer, Marion, TN

Securing Thread on Spools

When I've finished using a spool of thread, I place my finger against the spool and then wind the thread once around the spool and over my finger. I slip the free end under the loop, letting the end project a little, and pull to tighten. When I want thread from the spool, I give the free end a little tug and pull a length of thread from the spool. I cut off the length I need, leaving the remainder of the thread secured as before. No more thread snarls in my sewing basket or drawer!
Betty Jane Heacock, Westminster, MD

Securing Thread

Sorting Bobbins

Since I enjoy both quilting and fashion sewing, I find I have bobbins of both dual duty thread and quilting thread—usually in the same colors! To keep me from guessing which bobbin is which (and being too lazy to mark each bobbin), I have two bobbin cases, one marked "dual duty" and one marked "quilt piecing." This is very simple yet effective for any busy sewer.
Lois Klein, Wausau, WI

Candy Bobbins

I use an empty candy box (the kind with a plastic insert to keep each piece of candy separate) to store bobbins. Two or three bobbins fit in each candy compartment. If you sew with a friend or travel to a sewing class, just put the top on the box and away you go! (Of course, the best part is eating the candy.)
Kathy Gillis, Olympia, WA

Marked Bobbins

I keep bobbins in a small plastic box. To be certain I know the brand, the type, and the color of the thread, I write this information on the back of the bobbin with a permanent marker. I use a cotton swab and rubbing alcohol to remove the markings, and the bobbin can be used again and again.
Clarine Easley, Memphis, TN

Bobbin

Button Ice Trays

I organize my buttons using six plastic ice cube trays. I sort the buttons according to size and color and then store the trays in a drawer.
Doris Gossett, Overland Park, KS
Another idea: *Stephanie McMillian of Tallahassee, FL,* uses egg cartons the same way, decoupaging the cartons to make them more attractive.

Convenient Needle Threader

I bought a small hook attached to a suction cup and placed it on the front of my sewing machine. I then purchased a small wire needle threader and punched a hole in it. I hang the needle threader on the suction cup hook to keep the needle threader handy and to prevent it from falling down into the machine cabinet.
Christine Rust, Fort Wayne, IN

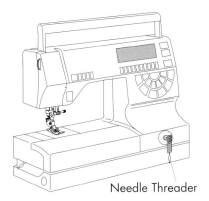

Needle Threader

Quick Thread Change

Most of my serging seems to involve light-colored fabrics and threads, but then along comes a pair of dark-colored slacks that need to be hemmed. I could change all three of my serger cones to a dark color, but I found an easier way. By changing only the needle thread and the upper looper thread and tightening the lower looper tension just enough so that it doesn't show (the most important step), only the dark thread shows on top. The one light thread is hidden underneath.
Phyllis Owen,
London, Ont., Canada

Thumbtack Needle Marker

I put my sewing machine needles into a tomato pincushion on which I have marked the various sections with different needle sizes. I saw this hint on your TV show, but I never remembered what size needle I had in the machine, so I came up with this idea: Whenever I remove a needle from the pincushion, I put a thumbtack (or colored head pin) in that section. Now all I have to do is look at my pincushion, and I know instantly which size needle I have in my machine. I also know that all the needles in the pincushion are used needles—even when I insert a new needle into my machine, I still put the tack into the appropriate section on the cushion.
Dorothy Bylin, Adams, ND

Tomato Pincushion

Candle Needle Holder

I'm a longtime sewer and novice quilter. When quilting I often lose needles. I now keep six to eight needles in a votive candle, using the candle as a pincushion. The wax coating helps the needles go in and out of the fabric easily, and I no longer lose the needles.
Beverly Reynolds, Brownsburg, IN

Eyeglasses Case

I use an old snap-closure eyeglasses case to store my hand-sewing supplies, including sewing eyeglasses, small scissors, a thimble, a small metal crochet hook, a needle threader, and a needle holder. Whenever I do any hand sewing, I have the necessities ready for use.
Vera Oelschlager, Fort Worth, TX

Shoulder Pad Pincushions

I finally found a use for discarded shoulder pads! Since I have numerous sewing and craft projects going all the time, it seemed as if I was forever looking for needles, pins, thread, etc. As I was tossing shoulder pads from one scrap bag to another, I got the idea of making them into individual pincushions.

I fold a pad in half and stitch along the curved side, forming a pocket. I put thread, small scissors, a thimble, a needle threader, and any other small notions I want inside the pocket. I use the padded outside part to hold a few straight pins and the correct needle for each project.

I now have pincushions for embroidery, quilting, needlepoint, and mending, plus one to keep at the ironing board. I stock each pincushion with the appropriate supplies so that it's handy for each project.
Cheryl Schmitz, Pensacola, FL

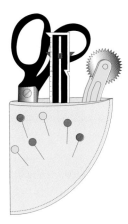

Shoulder Pad Pincushion

Empty Film Containers

I use empty plastic film holders to organize everything from bobbins and safety pins to hooks and eyes, snaps, buttons, and long quilting pins. The clear plastic containers are particularly useful for storing bobbins, since it is easy to see the color thread wound on each bobbin. I label all containers with masking tape to clearly identify items and sizes.
Jan Nilson, Vancouver, WA

Soap Pin Holder

To store all the pins I have for sewing, I stick them in a bar of soap. This helps the pins slide through fabric easily, and keeping the wrapper on the soap prevents the soap from crumbling.

Mildred O. Robertson, Baltimore, MD

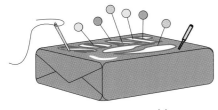

Soap Pin Holder

Fabric Sequin and Bead Holder

To store beads, sequins, snaps, hooks and eyes, skirt hooks, or anything else so small it tends to get lost in the shuffle, I took a piece of fabric (I used corduroy because it has a lot of body) about 22" (55.9-cm) wide and 34" (86.4-cm) long. I serged all four sides and then I made bar tacks 2" (5.1 cm) apart across and down the fabric using the sewing machine.

I fastened the fabric to the top of the sewing room closet door with thumbtacks and inserted paper clips or Christmas tree ornament hooks into the bar tacks. Then I purchased zip-top plastic bags in assorted sizes, punched holes in the tops, and hung them on the hooks. Everything stored in these bags is visible and easy to find.

Elizabeth Taylor, Arlington, TX

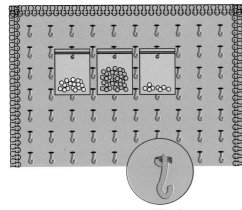

Organizer for Small Objects

Sewing Basket

I found that I needed a good-sized portable sewing basket, so I made one from a round basket that had never been used. I made a quilted lining with pockets to hold my necessary sewing items—pins, needles, thread, bobbins, tape measure, scissors, etc. I glued the lining into the basket and held the lining in place around the top edge, using clothespins until the glue dried. I still have room in the middle of the basket for large items and articles I'm working on.

I painted an attractive wreath of daisies and blueberries on the outside of the basket lid, as well as some additional designs inside the cover. This basket has served me well and still looks good after several years. It is so easy to carry this laden basket with one hand and my sewing machine with the other hand.

Thelma Tomlinson, Averill Park, NY

Tackle Box for Beads

I do a lot of crafts, and I always had a problem storing my leftover beads. Some were so small! One day my husband was organizing his tackle box to go fishing, and I realized a tackle box is a perfect container for many of the small items I have in my sewing room. His tackle box is small, but when I went to buy one, I found a lot of different sizes.

Gevelma Parker, Rome, GA

Fishing for Buttons

While buying fishing tackle for my boys, I discovered inexpensive little containers with screw-on lids intended for storing small pieces of fishing equipment. These are sold in units of six, and you can connect as many units as you want. I organize my buttons in these small jars by size and color. Since the containers are clear, I can look for a button without opening anything. The containers hardly take up any space, and I can get several buttons in each container.

Rita Heltsley, Sharon Grove, KY

On the Road

About that "portable" machine: when I take my machine with me, I use a luggage carrier.
Darlene Clark,
Largo, FL

Quicker "Reverse Sewing"

I make removing stitches quicker and easier by color-coding seams. When I use my 3/4-thread serger on a light-colored fabric, I use two or three white threads and one of beige or a light color. For dark-colored fabrics, I use black threads plus a single navy or dark brown. In my sewing machine, I put the beige or the navy thread in my bobbin.

Linda Brown,
Burleson, TX

Zippers on Hangers

To store zippers on hangers, I take plastic closures from bread or other food items and staple one to the top of each zipper. I twist the end of a closure to form a hook and slip it right over the hanger. You could also hang a dowel—¼" (6-mm) diameter or smaller—and use it like a small paper towel holder, hanging the zippers over the dowel.

Carol Henry, Erie, PA

Zip-top Organizers

My 10-year-old daughter, Colleen, is just learning to sew, and she likes to be organized. She came up with the idea of serging several zip-top plastic bags in a row onto a piece of fabric. Now she stores her thread, notions, and pattern pieces all together. This organizer can be hung or pinned near the sewing machine.

Rose and Colleen McGorey, Monroe, MI

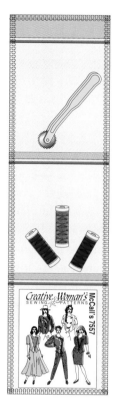

Zip-top Organizer

A Place (Mat) for Notions

Three matching place mats can easily become two sewing organizers—one for a gift and one for yourself, or one for your sewing room and another for travel.

Cut one place mat in half lengthwise and finish the cut edges with matching or coordinating bias tape or with a gathered ruffle. For one organizer, align the uncut edges and sew a half place mat to a full place mat around all but the cut edge. Stitch dividers to hold scissors, a rotary cutter, and your favorite notions. Roll up the completed organizer and tie it with ribbon, and you'll find that it fits into a small storage space or into a suitcase.

Mildred Hudson, Springtown, TX

PUTTING TOOLS AWAY

Easily keep scissors and other tools handy, inexpensively store your serger or sewing machine, and quickly find the instructions for all your tools!

Sewing Apron

So often my scissors, marking pens, and other accessories are hidden under pieces of fabric or roll off the table. I decided to make a sewing apron: I patterned it after a cooking apron but added pockets for all my tools. Now when I need something, I know right where it is—in my apron! Using the apron takes some getting used to, but once you get into the habit of returning everything to the pockets, it's really handy.

Ronnie Nichols, St. Louis, MO

Sewing Apron

Reference Books

I wanted to check one of my "Sewing With Nancy" series books for information about a certain technique, and it took me a long time to locate the book among the many others. There had to be a way to keep this reference book near my portable sewing machine!

I made a cloth cover to fit over my sewing machine cover, complete with pockets of various sizes. The side pocket is just right for my favorite sewing book. The other pockets accommodate other sewing notions such as scissors and measuring tape.

Carol McRight, Springdale, AR

Housewares Caddy

I stand a plastic tool or a housewares caddy next to my sewing machine to keep all my sewing tools upright and ready to grab. There are four divided sections for marking pens and pencils, seam guides and rippers, small scissors, and miscellaneous items. It's so convenient to have my tools at hand, plus the carrying handle makes it easy to move the caddy to my cutting table.

Lydia Sari, Marlton, NJ

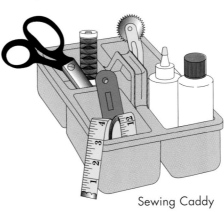

Sewing Caddy

Color-coded Scissors

When I was a child, my mother made clothes for our family (six children in all), and I knew I could always find sharp scissors for school projects in Mom's sewing box. Of course I didn't understand then why I shouldn't use them. Now that I sew, I realize how important it is to have very sharp scissors, and I've found a way to help families keep their scissors straight: color-code the scissors. I use red dots for my sewing scissors and green for family scissors. I place the dots by the adjustment screw, where they're easy for my children or husband to see. That way there's no question which scissors to use.

Aida Jaus, Poway, CA

Break for Sewing

Instead of coffee breaks, I take sewing breaks. I find these breaks relaxing, besides being productive.
M.J.G.,
Whitewater, WI

Sewing Break

Typed Labels

I make labels the easy way. It's possible to type anything on muslin or cotton fabrics. Then I just pink the edges of the labels, stitch around the edges with a fusible thread, and fuse each label in place.
Helen Edwards,
Perryville, KY

Gift Log

I sew a lot of gifts, and I have a large collection of fabrics and patterns for these projects. I record in a notebook which pattern and fabrics I used for each gift and to whom I gave it. Now I don't have to rely on my memory to avoid duplications, and I can intentionally give a gift that will complement one I've already given to that person. I also get a great sense of accomplishment from looking at the list of completed gifts.
Nancy Ferree,
Elk Creek, MO

Pot Holder for Scissors

This quick-and-easy scissors case keeps my shears handy and protects little hands from the sharp blades. I take a pot holder and position the loop at the top to serve as a hanger. After folding the pot holder into a cone shape, I handstitch the edges together. At the center top where the two sections overlap, I hot-glue or stitch ribbon, flowers, or other decorative trim in place.
Ruby Duncan, Hensley, AR

Pot Holder Scissors Case

Banded Scissors

When I finish using scissors or if I'm traveling and don't have a travel scissors case, I wrap a rubber band several times around the center of the closed blades until the rubber band is taut. I'm less likely to damage the scissors (or myself) if I drop them!
Joyce Dalton, Forest, VA

Cutting Mat

I have just begun to learn how to quilt and recently became the owner of a rotary cutter and a large cutting mat. Storing the mat can be a problem in a small house. I solved the problem by hanging the mat in the closet with a skirt hanger.
Sachiko Okada, Rancho Cordova, CA

Rotary Cutter Storage

I store my rotary cutter in an eyeglasses case.
Carol Fisher, Cleve Heights, OH

Machine Feet

Until I figured out a way to organize my sewing machine accessory feet, I didn't use the extra feet because I didn't know which was which, or which foot to use for special jobs. Then I placed a label on the top right corner of a small zip-top plastic bag (the heavier kind), showing the foot enclosed. I then put the foot itself into an even smaller bag, showing the name of the foot and the product number. For quick reference, I inserted a 3" x 5" (7.5-cm x 12.5-cm) card with the name of the foot at the top and a list of different uses for this particular foot, along with any tips or special instructions and sometimes a sample. If instructions or uses were available from books, I made a copy to include them. I keep these plastic bags together in a small basket so that I can quickly go through them when I need a special foot.
Jo Saal, Virginia Beach, VA

Pressing Tools

I sewed curtain rings onto my pressing ham and sleeve roll and screwed a cup hook into each wooden pressing tool so that I could store them on the Peg-Board that covers half of one of my sewing room walls. The pressing tools now hang on my wall within easy reach of my ironing board.
Doreen Stewart, Shenandoah Junction, WV

Peg-Board Organizer

Serger Table

To store my serger, I made a simple modification to a horizontal file cabinet, available in kit form from most local variety discount stores. I assembled the file cabinet following the manufacturer's directions with two exceptions: I did not install the file folder hanging rods on the inside of the cabinet, and I left off the top hinge cover rods.

The cover rods keep the top from moving past the vertical position, so leaving them off permitted the top to swing over far enough to provide a shelf. I cut a 1"-thick (2.5-cm-thick) piece of wood and mounted it to the back side of the cabinet with hinges. This swings out to support the top/shelf. I store the serger inside the cabinet and put it on this shelf to use it.

To prevent the cabinet from tipping when the serger is positioned on the shelf, I wrapped a towel around a brick and basted the open edges closed. Several covered bricks go on the bottom shelf to counterbalance the serger.

Harvey Foushee, Robbinsville, NJ

Serger Table

Nonslip Hanger Covers

Many garments slide every which way on hangers, so I found a way to make simple hanger covers using fabric scraps. I prefer to use pile or fleece fabric or even thin sponge rubber. (I use the sponge rubber for silk blouses—it leaves no creases or marks at the shoulder.)

I cut a 3"-wide (7.5 cm-wide) fabric strip about 1½" (3.8 cm) shorter than the top of the hanger, with fabric stretching lengthwise, and then cut a ¾" (1.8-cm) slit in the center of the fabric for inserting the hanger hook. I fold the fabric in half lengthwise, right sides together, and sew the two ends. Presto! I have an easy-to-make cover that stretches just enough to stay securely on the hanger.

Mary Richardson, Seattle, WA

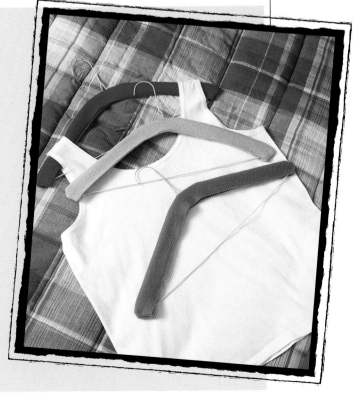

NOTIONS

For people who sew, a store with notions is a lot like a candy store is for kids—you want two of everything in sight!

Colorful thread, decorative buttons, elastic in different sizes and shapes—having the right notions on hand makes any sewing project quicker and helps you create a professional-looking project. Sometimes that "right notion" may be a substitute from your pantry or laundry room.

"Sewing With Nancy" viewers provide a wealth of hints for unusual ways to use everything from buttonhole space tape to coffee filters.

THREAD

Make this most basic sewing notion easier to use and save money at the same time!

Retirement Creed

To sew whatever I want
To sew whenever I want
To sew for whomever
I want
(Or until I run
out of thread!)
Ramona Ruggeri,
Norris, Il

Honey of a Hint

I keep a bobbin of beeswax-coated thread handy for quick hand-sewing jobs. I appreciate the added strength beeswax provides, and I save time and frustration because my thread does not tangle as easily. To apply beeswax, I put a bobbin on the machine, start winding the thread, and hold the beeswax under the thread as it unwinds from the spool. Presto! The thread is coated.
Laura Kight, Auburn, WA

Softer Thread

I prevent thread from tangling or knotting while hand-sewing by running the thread along a sheet of fabric softener before I begin to sew. I always keep a sheet with my sewing supplies.
Sharon Piechowiak, Apache Junction, AZ

Transparent Needle Thread

Cones of serging thread are expensive, especially when I need three spools of each color. To save money (and also to save time in changing colors), I use Wonder Thread or other transparent thread in my needle. This also lets me immediately identify the needle thread to pull if I have to take out a seam. Transparent thread works on all weights of fabric and looks no different from having three matching threads.
Lois Keenan, Green Valley, AZ

Other ideas: *Irene Mashburn of St. Cloud, FL,* uses transparent nylon thread in her sewing machine bobbin so that she doesn't have to change bobbins each time she changes thread spools. She notes that nylon thread doesn't show, even on dark fabric. *Josephine Heuertz of Springfield, MO,* takes this idea one step further by keeping her machine spool and bobbin threaded with very fine nylon colorless thread at all times. This way she's ready for any sewing jobs without searching for the correct color of thread.

Note from Nancy

Lingerie/bobbin thread (a braided stretchy thread) is also ideal for the bobbin. The special twist in this thread creates some stretch as you sew. This stretch draws the top thread to the underside, so that the bobbin thread remains hidden. Many alteration shops use transparent nylon thread to hem pants and skirts. One caution: Keep in mind that the thread is nylon, and a hot iron could melt it.

A Revealing Hint

Invisible thread (such as Wonder Thread) is great when I don't want the thread to be seen, but it's frustrating to try to thread a machine or hand needle with invisible thread. I use a felt-tip permanent black marker to color the last ½" (1.3 cm) of the thread so that I can see to put it through the eye of the needle. I put the thread end on a small piece of paper or cardboard and then mark the end with the pen. By marking the thread before putting the spool away, I can easily find the thread end the next time I use it.

Jean McKay, San Diego, CA

Tandem Tensions

To serge a rolled edge on a napkin, I wanted to combine woolly nylon and rayon threads in the upper looper. I was unable to adjust the tensions correctly to establish a smooth finish until it occurred to me that since I was using only one needle, the right needle tension slot was empty. I threaded the rayon through that tension slot, adjusting the tension a little tighter than for the woolly nylon. Then I brought the thread down to a point where it could join the woolly nylon to be threaded into the upper looper. The stitch created a smooth rolled edge with the variegated look I wanted.

Jane Clark, New Port Richey, FL

Take Your Time

If you wind your bobbin at a slow speed, the thread winds more easily and evenly and will not pucker or break when sewing.

Helen Kronenberg, Beaver Dam, WI

Nancy's Notions Humble Beginning

In 1979, I began free-lancing, giving seminars for fabric stores and educational groups. At each seminar, I passed out an 8½" x 11" flyer created at my kitchen table. The flyer featured a handful of sewing books and notions. I called the sheet **Nancy's Notions**.

About a year and a half later, after moving to Beaver Dam, Wisconsin, I acquired two employees: my in-laws. We worked out of my basement to produce a 12-page catalog. Shortly after our move, I began my own cable TV show, "Sewing With Nancy." The show gave **Nancy's Notions**, the program's only sponsor, great exposure.

My father-in-law renovated their 1000-square-foot "chicken house" in 1983 into **Nancy's Notions** first warehouse, complete with carpet and air conditioning--the chickens never had it so good! My husband, Richard, joined me full-time that year. Our next move came in 1985 to a remodeled 6,000-square-foot distribution center. Two and a half years later our growth led us to our current 49,000-square-foot building. We process 500 to 2000 mail orders daily from our 164-page catalog--a far cry from my first 8½" x 11" flyer.

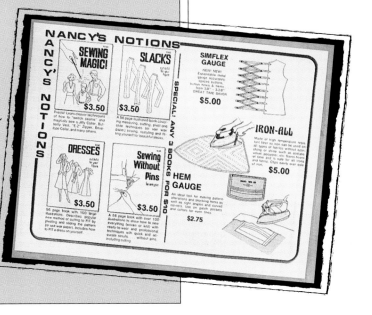

Keep a Diary

One New Year's Day, I began a sewing diary, keeping a list of every sewing or mending project for the year. Reading through it on the next New Year's Day was a rewarding experience and a pleasant trip down memory lane. Since then I've expanded this diary to include pattern numbers and sizes, fabrics, fitting notes, and other comments. This is especially helpful because I sew for many children and grandchildren who live in other towns. But the best part is my feeling of accomplishment.
Barbara DeWeese, Zionsville, IN

Spool/Cone Combo

Late one night when I was working on a banner that I had to have finished in the morning for a customer, I ran out of black sewing machine thread. I inserted a spool of thread (you could use an empty spool) inside a cone of black serger thread and fit the thread combo onto the spindle of my sewing machine. It worked perfectly!
Debbie McKrisky, Lower Burrell, PA

Spool/Cone Combo

Cones for Sewing

I use an empty glass coffee jar with a plastic lid to hold serger thread for use on a regular sewing machine. My husband drilled a small hole in the lid to dispense the thread. I place the jar containing the thread on my sewing table behind my machine, pull the thread up through the hole in the lid, and thread my machine as usual.

I have cones of different sizes, so I have jars to match the two most popular size cones. They work as well as purchased serger thread cone holders.
Jean Martin, Sedona, AZ

Crocheted and Fused

I loved to use ThreadFuse (fusible thread) but wasn't always pleased with the results. Now I use fusible thread to crochet a chain, using a size 7 or 9 crochet hook. I zigzag the chain onto my project and fuse, and it stays forever. The crocheted chain gives more coverage, which means it holds better. I hem slacks, place mats, and quilt bindings this way.
Joan Demanette, Concordia, KS

Three for One

Serging with matching thread can be too expensive when it means buying four cones of thread that you know you'll probably never use up. My solution is to buy one cone of thread and fill six bobbins.

The simplest way to wind the bobbins is to put the cone on the serger where the upper looper cone belongs, pull the thread over to the sewing machine, and connect it to the bobbin winder.

To serge, thread the upper looper with cone thread and remove the plastic cone holders from the other spindles. Then put one bobbin on each of the other spindles. (If you're using four threads, use three bobbins and set the other three aside.) Put a small spool of serger thread on top of each bobbin to hold it in place, thread each bobbin as if it were a cone of thread, and serge as usual!

What are the extra bobbins for? When you run out of thread in the bobbins, simply replace them with the extras.
Marilyn Hunt, Post Falls, ID, and Elaine Duke, Mobile, AL

Serger Bobbins

Dental Floss Threader

I use a dental floss threader (available in most drug stores and many grocery stores) to thread my overlock machine. It goes through those holes slick as a whistle.
A.R., Omaha, NE

A Knotty Problem

I love to use my serger, but it always took me a very long time to change thread spools. My first problem was that when I pulled threads through the threading sequences, the knots would come apart. I had to finish threading by hand with tweezers (*very* time consuming). Now I tie both ends of the threads together in a single knot, and these don't come apart.

My second problem resulted from following the serger manufacturer's directions to pull each individual thread through the serger one at a time by hand. This means I had to pull the thread with one hand while holding the tension knob with the other. Because the eyes of both loopers are much larger than the needle eyes, the threads slipped right through.

I solved this by using my presser foot while changing thread. The serger chainstitches as usual, and knots slip right through the loopers. Because the needle thread advances slowly compared with the looper threads, I can make a chain until the new needle thread is just above the needle and clip the threads according to the instructions. I then thread the needle using tweezers and the new thread color before serging a few inches to complete the chain.
Marianne Mackey-Smith, Tampa, FL

Double Thread Knots

When hand-sewing buttons, hems, etc., I prefer doubled thread for strength but don't like the big knot necessary to hold the thread in place. Instead I double my thread and thread the two ends through the eye of the needle. Then I can catch the loop on the underside, creating a smooth finish.
Kathleen Shubert, Menomonee Falls, WI
Another idea: *Frances Mabry of Karnes City, TX,* threads her needle in the conventional way but separately knots each strand. She says she's been surprised by how few tangles she has when using this method.

Ouija Knots

When I was a milliner in San Francisco, we used a special ouija knot for all hand sewing, especially for attaching veiling to hats. To make a ouija knot, take a small stitch, wrap one end of the thread around the needle, and then wrap the other end of the thread around the needle in the other direction. Pull the needle through, and the ouija knot will never pull out.

When I sew on buttons, I take a tiny stitch on the top fabric with doubled thread, exactly where I want to put the button. Then I sew on the button (not too tightly) and wrap the thread around the stitches to form a little shank. I finish with a ouija knot right under the button. No knots show on the wrong side.
Irene Myers, Graeagle, CA

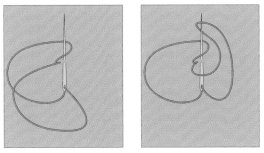

Ouija Knot

Threading Yarn

I found a fast and easy way to thread yarn through the eye of a needle: Wrap a piece of transparent tape snugly over the end of the yarn, cut the tape to a point, and thread it through the needle. After the yarn is through the eye of the needle, cut off the tape-wrapped end. This works great when I'm making craft items, knitting, tying quilts, etc.
Eve Stanfill, Houston, TX

Notions for Kids

To keep my daughter busy while I sew—a real challenge—I bought a large plastic sewing box in her favorite color and filled it with "notions" I found around the house (empty thread spools, large thimbles, a plastic ruler, and fabric and trim swatches). I also put in a pincushion (no pins), a tape measure, and a toy iron.

Next I took several boxes of different sizes and glued them together in the shape of a sewing machine, adding details like the needle and the thread with a marker.
Pamela Horvath, Manchester, CT

INTERFACINGS AND STABILIZERS

What do you do at midnight when you've run out of stabilizer and need to finish machine-embroidering your daughter's dance recital costume? "Sewing With Nancy" viewers help solve that and other problems.

Dry-Away Your Wash-Away

When I don't wish to completely wet an article to remove Wash-Away stabilizer, I wet a towel, wring it out well by hand, and place both the towel and my finished project in the clothes dryer. After the project has tumbled for a few minutes on low heat, all the residue of the Wash-Away is removed by the humidity from the wet towel in the hot dryer.
Wanda Baker,
Harrison, AK

A Dryer Idea

To back appliqués with another fabric layer, stitch around the layers, leaving an opening for turning, and then turn them right side out before sewing them to a project. Interfacing works well as this second layer, but it can be expensive. Used fabric softener sheets (from the clothes dryer) work well, and this is a great way to recycle them.
Juanita Tilton, Fayetteville, AR,
and Lucille Martin, Vinita, OK
Another idea: *Theresa Stephan of Grand Prairie, TX,* stores her old fabric softener sheets in a bag in her sewing room. She uses them to stabilize buttonholes and decorative trims, as well as for appliqués.

Ready-to-Fuse Appliqués

To use fusible interfacing as a second layer on appliqués, first trace the design on the non-fusible side of the interfacing. Then place the fusible side of the interfacing on the right side of the appliqué fabric and stitch around the entire design. Next trim the seam allowances to ⅛" (3 mm) and make a slit in the interfacing. When you turn the appliqué right side out, all raw edges are on the inside, and the fusible part of the interfacing is on the outside of the back. You can position the appliqué where you want it and press, holding the appliqué in place for stitching.

When you work with sheer fashion fabric or want to avoid adding bulk to an appliqué, simply use a water-soluble stabilizer such as Wash-Away instead of fusible interfacing. After you turn the design and stitch it in place, dissolve the stabilizer for a perfect appliqué.
Pat White, Collierville, TN,
and Sharon Smith, Walkersville, MD

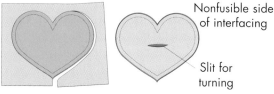

Nonfusible side of interfacing

Slit for turning

Fusible Appliqués

Wonder-Under Note Cards

A little fusible web turns paper, fabric, and ribbon scraps into unique greeting cards that are so easy they're great projects for young children, scout groups, or other youth organizations! I iron Wonder-Under fusible web on the wrong side of a fabric, choose a design, and trace it onto the paper side of the Wonder-Under. I cut out the designs, iron them onto a plain note card, and I'm done.
Lisa Bendler, Wauwatosa, WI

Recycled Plastic Bags

Bond fabric for appliqués using ordinary plastic bags from the dry cleaner. First center a piece of plastic slightly larger than the appliqué between the appliqué and the base fabric. Then place a brown paper sack on top of the appliqué and press with a hot iron. Any excess plastic adheres to the sack. The appliqué stays firmly in place while you satin-stitch or blind-stitch the edges. Make sure to completely cover the plastic with the brown sack to avoid getting plastic stuck to the iron soleplate.
Barb Gourd, Des Moines, IA; Jeanne Mason, Orem, UT; and M.J. Davis, Seattle, WA

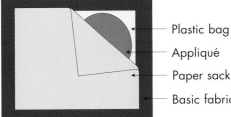

Bonding with Plastic Bags

Note from Nancy
An appliqué bonded in this fashion will not be as secure as one bonded with fusible web, but it will provide an adequate bond if the appliqué is also stitched after fusing. I've found this technique works best if you trim the plastic as closely as possible to the size of the appliqué; otherwise, you may see a slight plastic residue around the edges of the design after you complete the project. What an innovative way to recycle plastic laundry bags!

Coffee Break
When you get a sudden urge to do free-motion-embroidery but find you're out of stabilizer, just grab a coffee filter. It fits well in a round embroidery hoop and makes a great substitute for commercial stabilizers. Keep a package of filters in your sewing room.
Nell Caldwell, Oklahoma City, OK, and Kam McCabe, Waukesha, WI

Liquid Alternative
I like to machine-embroider but find liquid stabilizers (such as Perfect Sew) too expensive, so I use hair spray. It dries very fast (using a hair dryer makes it dry even faster), works like expensive liquid stabilizers, and costs just pennies.
Dorothy Hanson, Melbourne, FL

Note from Nancy
The liquid stabilizer Perfect Sew is applied to the fabric, dried, and then sewn with decorative stitches; it washes out completely. Before using hair spray on your garment, be sure to test it on a sample. Various brands of hair spray differ in their chemical compositions, and some may change the color or the appearance of a fabric, especially acetate or lining fabrics. To be safe, always test. You'd rather be safe than sorry!

Another idea: *Mary Stevens of Lady Lake, FL,* uses heavy spray starch to stabilize washable fabrics before adding decorative stitches. Two or three applications of starch make the fabric firm enough for stitching to lie flat without puckering, and there's no tear-away stabilizer to pick out of intricate designs such as honeycomb. Regular laundering removes the starch.

Note from Nancy
What a great idea! We've found that applying several light coats of starch and pressing between each coat gives better results than saturating the fabric with one heavy coat of starch. You can make the fabric very stiff, and decorative stitches will look smooth and even. (Remember, this works only for washable fabrics.)

Net a Crisp Bow
The bridesmaids' dresses I made for my son's wedding included large bows, and I needed to be certain that the bows looked crisp and didn't roll or fold over. I backed the garment fabric with nylon net and treated the two layers as one when I sewed the bow. This made the fabric very stable, and the bows looked perky and perfect.
Ruth DuCharme, Baker, MT

Storing Fusibles
Keep Wonder-Under and HeatnBond in plastic bags so that they don't dry out.
Peg Schubert, Milwaukee, WI

BUTTONS

These practical fasteners can also be great decorative elements.

Button Party

Since I've had a stroke, I have some difficulty sewing small items such as buttons and snaps. So I host a "finish party"—I invite friends over to sew on the small items, and I serve something they love to eat. We have lots of fun looking over what we've been able to do and just talking.
Jayne Tepper, Columbus, OH

Handy Spare

You're away from home, and a button comes off. What can you do? I sew a spare button to a safety pin and then pin it to the garment where it cannot be seen. If a button comes off, I pin the spare in place and button up. Later, when I have access to a needle and thread, I sew the spare to the garment.
Elvera Gutierrez, Sunnyvale, CA

Matching Buttons to Fabric

When I take a sample of fabric to the store to buy buttons, I cut a small slit in it about the size of the buttonhole I plan to use. When I find a button I think might work, and it's attached to a white card (which throws off the way I see the color), I slip the fabric around the button and can see perfectly how well it matches.
Ruth Carr, Overland Park, KS

Heavy-duty Button Thread

I use dental floss to sew on buttons that are going to get rough handling (such as on children's wear and sports clothes).
Barbara Meyers, Bolingbrook, IL
Other ideas: *Joan Ochs of Fort Lee, NJ*, uses eight-strand embroidery floss to sew on buttons. Two stitches secure a button. Joan stores embroidery floss left over from craft projects on café curtain rings. *Ida Davenport of San Jose, CA*, likes the sturdiness and durability of Wonder Thread or other monofilament thread for sewing on metal shank buttons, but she had trouble making a knot in the thread. Now she combines a strand of all-purpose sewing thread with a strand of monofilament thread in the needle and has no trouble making knots.

Smooth Buttonholes

I use Fray Check liquid seam sealant on my buttonholes to prevent fraying.
Elisabeth Walts, Lafayette, CA

Corded Buttonholes

To make a corded buttonhole, I serge about an 8" (20-cm) thread tail. When I pull this tail taut, it hooks into the front and back toes of my buttonhole foot and makes a great buttonhole cording. When the buttonhole is complete, I pull the tails to get rid of the loop; then I tie and clip the ends.
Jill Thomas, Potsdam, NY

Cutting Buttonholes

For perfect buttonholes, I use the following technique: After sewing a buttonhole, I place the fabric on a hard surface, such as a counter, and run the dull edge of a good-quality seam ripper between the lines of stitching two or three times on both sides of the fabric. (This provides a track for the seam ripper to follow.) I push the point of the ripper into one end of the buttonhole to make a small cut, turn the buttonhole around to the other end, and push in the seam ripper again. Holding the fabric taut, I slide the seam ripper almost to the end of the buttonhole, ease the point through the hole, and cut.
Anne Turner, Bothell, WA

A Black Hole

After cutting open a buttonhole on a black wool jacket, the white interfacing was visible between the layers of fabric. I took a permanent black fabric marker and colored the interfacing to match the jacket. With the availability of multicolored permanent markers, this tip would work well for any color of garment.
Kimberly Schell, Fayetteville, NC, and Katherine Ewell, Manchester, TN

Note from Nancy
Make sure you use fabric markers.

Spare Covered Buttons

When making covered buttons, I cut out two or three extra circles of fabric for each garment and keep these circles with an extra uncovered button of that size in a zip-top plastic bag. If I lose a button from a garment, I can quickly make a replacement without searching through all my fabric scraps, but I haven't spent time making extra buttons that I may never need.
Connie DeWitt, Magazine, AR

Tear-Away Buttonhole Marks

My machine doesn't have an automatic setting for the length of a buttonhole, so I have to mark the buttonhole length on the fabric. Some fabrics don't lend themselves to marking, and while I can usually locate a buttonhole starting mark under the presser foot, I often had trouble seeing the stopping point. Now I pin a narrow strip of paper exactly at the stopping point and add a straight mark to help me guide the buttonhole line. It's so simple to stop at precisely the right spot. I can use a single paper strip along the length of all the buttonholes (which helps work out overall buttonhole placement) or use individual strips for each buttonhole.
Ruth Hafemeister, Leavenworth, KS

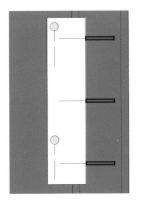

Buttonhole Stopping Point

Easy Button Loops

The directions for a project I was making called for ⅛"-wide (3 mm-wide) elastic button loops. I didn't want to use white elastic on my colored sweatshirt, so I tried ¼"-wide (6-mm-wide) clear elastic—it worked great! I pulled the elastic up through the opening in a Teflon presser foot (the Teflon coating helps elastic or vinyl glide easily under the foot), stretching the elastic slightly, so that it rolled toward the center. I satin-stitched over the elastic with thread matched to the garment, making ⅛"-wide (3-mm-wide) finished loops. Then I cut the elastic into the 1½"-long (3.75-mm-long) pieces I needed and applied Fray Check seam sealant to the ends. The results were strong, good-looking loops.
Beverly Lovan, Winter Haven, FL

Blindhemming Button Loops

I use elastic thread and a blindhem foot to make button loops for little girls' dresses and for bridal or evening wear. I place elastic thread along the outer edge of the buttonhole area and secure it to the fabric using the blindhem stitch, which consists of a straightstitch combined with a zigzag stitch. The straightstitch goes on the edge of the fabric, and the zigzag catches the thread. Tiny buttons fit through the elastic loops. I make sure to catch the elastic securely at the top and the bottom of the seam.
K.S., Anaheim, CA

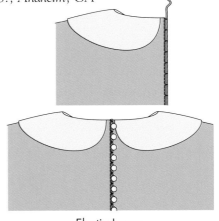

Elastic Loops

Recycled Button Loops

For button loops, I use the elastic cords I cut off after I make a garment with Stitch 'n Stretch. I use thread that matches my garment and sew over the cords several times with a short zigzag stitch before attaching them to the garment. These loops not only look nice, but they also slip over the buttons easier and are much faster to make than hand-sewn button loops. I wish I had known to do this a few months ago when I needed almost 100 loops for bridesmaids' dresses I was making! (I also use this technique for belt loops for dresses.)
Bonnie Loyd, Arnold, MO

Note from Nancy

If you don't have cords from Stitch 'n Stretch available, you could use pieces of elastic thread for this technique. It's an easy way to have loops exactly the right color.

Couture Buttonholes

For my sister's wedding, I wanted to dress up the matching jacket of an elegant but very plain dress. The pattern called for button closures at the back of the jacket and on the cuffs. I thought that lace with an open weave would be nice with little pearl or baby buttons. The lace became decorative, ready-made buttonholes. Later I found that eyelet can be used in the same way, such as down the front of a little girl's dress.
Vicky Kennedy, Pomona, NJ

Lace Buttonholes

Embellished Covered Buttons

When using purchased covered button forms, I cut a fabric strip equal to the width indicated on the package instructions and back the fabric with a stabilizer such as Stitch-N-Tear (tear-away stabilizer). I select one of my machine's decorative stitches and sew this design down the center of the fabric strip. I cut out the circles for covering the buttons and then proceed according to the package instructions. Voilà! Great-looking buttons!
Julia Miller,
Randallstown, MD

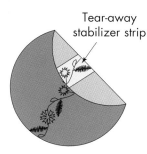

Tear-away stabilizer strip

Personalized Covered Buttons

Recycling Buttonhole Markers

I'm a Maine Yankee who hates to waste anything, so I use a single narrow strip of tear-away stabilizer to mark buttonholes on three garments.

Using a piece of stabilizer a few inches longer than the garment I'm sewing, I mark the neckline and the hemline and then mark the buttonholes. Then I draw the same markings a second time about 1" or 1½" (2.5 cm to 3.8 cm) away from the first markings, using a different color pen and numbering these with a "2." I mark another set 1" to 1½" (2.5 cm to 3.8 cm) away in a third color and number these with a "3."

After I use the first markings, I store the stabilizer in the pattern envelope, and I'm ready for the next garment. It saves time and stabilizer, and I get perfect buttonholes every time.
Ramona Meserve, Bowdoinham, ME

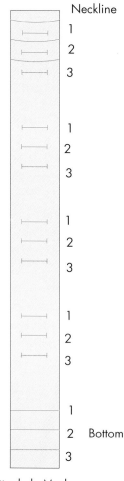

Neckline
1
2
3

1
2
3

1
2
3

1
2
3

1
2 Bottom
3

Buttonhole Markers

Ultrasuede Covered Buttons

To make Ultrasuede covered buttons, I start with common flat two-hole buttons. For each covered button, I cut two squares of fusible web larger than the button and two squares of Ultrasuede larger than the webbing. After I fuse the web to the wrong side of the Ultrasuede, I sandwich the button between the two pieces of Ultrasuede (web sides toward the button), and place the button sandwich on a folded towel. Then I fuse the layers together, using a damp press cloth and a moderately heated iron. I remove the cloth, finger-press to shape the Ultrasuede around the button, and let the button cool.

I thread a needle with about 24" (60 cm) of doubled thread, bring the needle through one hole of the covered button, and take a small stitch. With the thread on the underside of the button, I go under the Ultrasuede to the outer edge of the button. Then I make small backstitches around the outside of the button, stitching as close to the button as possible. When finished, I slide the needle under the Ultrasuede and back to the center of the button. After trimming the Ultrasuede to button size, I use the same thread to stitch the button to the garment.
Barbara Miller, Bucyrus, OH

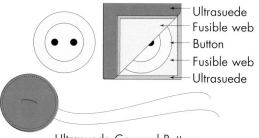

Ultrasuede
Fusible web
Button
Fusible web
Ultrasuede

Ultrasuede Covered Buttons

Fuse Covered Buttons

I back the fabric that I use to cover buttons with Wonder-Under fusible web and then draw circles of the required size on the paper side of the Wonder-Under. It's so much easier to draw circles on the paper backing after it's been applied to the fabric than it is to draw on the fabric itself. The web gives the fabric some sturdiness (without bulk) plus a little stickiness and pliability when wrapping the fabric onto the button.
Cindy Dworetsky, Englewood, CO

Removable Buttons

Last year I bought a suit that included a white jacket with a single large blue button. I like to mix and match my clothes and I felt very restricted by that blue button. I removed the button and made a ½" (1.3-cm) buttonhole where the it had been. Then I chose several large buttons, each of which matched a skirt that I wanted to wear with the jacket. I sewed ½" (1.3-cm) buttons to the backs of the larger buttons, allowing a generous shank between the two buttons. The jacket is now a lot more versatile.
Jacquelyn Parkinson, Honolulu, HI
Other ideas: *Maria Abaunza of Miami Lakes, FL*, saves the pins from cards of buttons. She makes a ¼"-long (6-mm-long) mini button-hole in matching thread on the garment where the button should be, inserts the shank into the hole, and secures the button with the pin. The button stays attached yet is easily replaced in seconds. *Inez Anthony of Jackson, MS*, keeps heavy shank buttons from weighing down and distorting clothes by making the shank buttons removable.

Buttonhole Chart

If your sewing machine has many different sizes and styles of automatic buttonholes, make a sample of each buttonhole (including cutting it open), mark the sizes, and hang the samples on the wall behind the machine. When you need to find the correct size buttonhole for a particular button, pass the button through each sample until you find the correct size and style. This chart saves a lot of time and frustration.
*Michele Hunter, Waukegan, IL,
and Charlotte Dauffenbach, Stillwater, MN*
Another idea: To avoid having to juggle the zigzag-stitch width to find the right width for each new button she wants to sew on by machine, *Mary Hardenbrook of Huntington Beach, CA*, used an old, large, unthreaded needle to sew each width onto an ordinary index card. When she's ready to sew on a button, she places the button on the template until she finds the right width. It's even more accurate when she holds the button and the template up to light.

Machine Needles for Button Shanks

When my sewing machine needles become dull, I keep them in a pincushion and use them to form thread shanks when I sew on two- or four-hole buttons. The tailor tack foot for my sewing machine sometimes forms too long a shank, so I insert a machine needle a little over ¼" (6 mm) away from the button mark, place the button over the needle, and sew the button in place, either by machine or by hand.

The needle stays in place until I remove it by pushing on the point with a thimble. If you have as many dull needles as I do, you can put a needle at each button mark and remove them when all the buttons are sewn in place. Or you can move one needle from mark to mark as each button is sewn on.
Melanie Walker, Odessa, TX

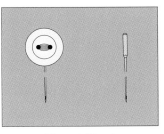

Thread Shanks

Elastic Buttonhole Stabilizer

Before I stitch buttonholes, I place small pieces of clear elastic (left over from other projects) between the facing and the fashion fabric. The elastic keeps the buttonholes from stretching out of shape.
Virginia Regelin, Tarpon Springs, FL

Shank Button Eyes

To keep shank buttons in place (particularly on coats or other garments where a lost button might be difficult to replace) use the eye from a hook-and-eye set. Put the eye through the button shank and mark the placement for the eye. Then remove the button and stitch one side of the eye in place. Finally slide the button on the shank and stitch the remaining side.
*Norma Lober, Baltimore, MD,
and Joanne Cullen, Omaha, NE*

Polished Buttons

I keep a bottle of clear nail polish in the sewing box. When I buy or make a new garment, I touch the center of each button with the polish to seal the threads so that they won't unravel. It's a lifesaver for boys' and men's shirts!
Pearl Harrison,
Franklin, KY

ELASTIC

Stretch your imagination with some of these handy hints on attaching, covering, and using elastic.

Scarf Belts with Elastic Stabilizer

I cut a piece of 1¼"- or 1½"-wide (3.1-cm- or 3.75-cm-wide) nonroll elastic equal to the length of my waist measurement, tapering the ends with scissors before applying Fray Check seam sealant. I fold the scarf I want to use in a triangle and center the elastic along the folded edge. When I wrap the scarf around the elastic and then tie the scarf around my waist, the scarf can't scrunch.
Barbara Tuttle, Beaverton, OR

Bartacking Elastic

When sewing elastic to a sleeve, I bar-tack the elastic to the garment at the beginning, the end, and the middle. Then, when I zigzag the elastic in place, the elastic is divided evenly and I have no difficulty holding the ends in place. *Vivian Cashatt, Grants Pass, OR*

Color-coding with Pins

I have a little trick I do with colored head pins when quartering a neckline or a cuff to add a collar or ribbing. I use a red pin at the center back, a yellow one at the center front, and a white one at the shoulder seam. This helps me know which is which when I put the collar or the ribbing onto the garment. *Pat Stapleton, Albuquerque, NM*

Holding Elastic in a Pinch

While sewing a pretty dress for my daughter, I stitched ⅛"-wide (3-mm-wide) elastic across each short sleeve before attaching it to the bodice, stretching the elastic as I sewed. At the end of each sleeve, I could no longer stretch the elastic with my fingers because they were at the point of touching the presser foot. I fetched my eyebrow tweezers and used them to hold and stretch the elastic right to the edge of the sleeve as I sewed. Now the tweezers stay in my sewing box for this use. *Rhonda Schneckenburger, Morrisburg, Ont., Canada*

Note from Nancy
You can also use serger tweezers!

Freestanding Casing

I've always felt that the line of stitching you see on the outside of a garment with an elastic waistline really marks it as homemade. To avoid this line, I make a minor adjustment, creating a casing in the seam allowance rather than making a pocket for elastic between the bodice and the skirt.

Usually the seam allowance between the bodice and the skirt (or pants, if it's a jumpsuit) is ¾" (1.8 cm) wide. To create a casing for ½"-wide (1.3-cm-wide) elastic, I stitch the seam allowances together at the seam line and again ⅛" (3 mm) from the raw edge. This makes a freestanding casing for elastic. After I finish the raw edge with a zigzag stitch, I insert the elastic through the casing, adjust the gathers so that they're even around the garment. To ensure that the elastic stays in place (with the seam allowance pressed toward the hem) I stitch in-the-ditch at the side seams and the center back or front (if applicable).

My elastic doesn't shift, the gathers don't bunch up on one side of the garment, and I don't get the telltale line of topstitching on the right side of my garment.
Peggy Warren, Gloucester, Ont., Canada

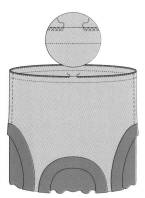

Invisible Elastic Casing

Covering Sew-Through Elastic

I wanted a way to completely cover sports elastic for a pattern with an elasticized waist in a separate waistband. I cut the elastic, aligned the edge of the elastic with the center of the waistband, extended ends ¼" (6 mm) into the seam allowances and stitched both ends. Stretching the elastic to meet the fabric, I sewed along the elastic's grooves. Next I folded over the fabric, meeting the cut edges, and restitched along the first rows of stitches. Finally I stitched the center back seam of the waistband and then stitched the waistband to the skirt, using the side that had been stitched only once as the right side.

It came out great! Many of my friends wanted my secret. This should also work with patterns where the waistband is not separate. Just cut it separately, adding appropriate seam allowances.
Michelle Lane, Sedona, AZ

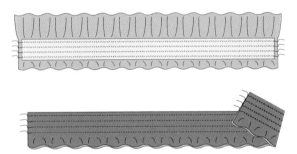

Covered Elastic Waistband

Note from Nancy
Wide sports elastic has four unbraided rows that serve as guidelines when stitching.

Gathering Before Attaching

Sometimes when using elastic to gather a much wider piece of fabric, I have over-stretched the elastic, making it lose its stretch. To prevent this, I gather the material somewhat before attaching it to the elastic. This lets me maintain the stretch of the elastic.
Betty Laiblin, Seattle, WA

Double Bodkins

When inserting elastic into a casing, I use two bodkins, one on each end of the elastic. If I pull too far and lose one end, I can easily find it without having to remove the elastic completely and start over. This is quicker for me than pinning one end to the opening before I begin to insert the other end of the elastic.
Belva Barrick, Glendale, AZ

Note from Nancy
A bodkin is a notion similar to tweezers, with special teeth to grip elastic and pull it through a casing.

Free Bodkins

To easily insert elastic into a casing, I use a garbage bag plastic closure and an extralong piece of elastic. First I trim the sides and round the tip of the closure so that it slides through the casing more easily. Then, rather than cutting the elastic to the needed length, I use a very long piece of elastic.

With narrow elastics, I pass one end of the elastic through the opening of the plastic closure, fold it over, and stitch the elastic to itself. With wider pieces of elastic, I cut a yard of bias tape, stitch the elastic to the tape, thread the tape through the plastic closure, and stitch the tape to itself.

I mark how much elastic I need for the garment, pull the elastic to the marked position, and cut at the marked length. By marking and cutting from the end opposite the plastic closure, I only have to sew the elastic to the plastic "bodkin" once. The remaining elastic is ready to thread through the next casing.
Jill Mount, Falmouth, VA

Crosshatch Joining

When joining elastic, I use the crosshatch (darning) stitch on my machine to sew the ends of the elastic together. This makes a very secure and flat joint.
Anne Johnson, Winnipeg, Man., Canada

Drawstring Bags Organize Sewing

I make drawstring cloth bags and store notions such as zippers, elastics, trims, and interfacing. I label the bags with whatever's inside and then store each bag on a hook or in a box.

I use these bags for more than sewing supplies. I've found drawstring bags to be the best dresser drawer dividers or suitcase organizers I could ever want. I have them in all colors, shapes, and sizes. These bags also make wonderful wraps to store toys and serve as gift wrappings.
Alice Huff,
Duncanville, TX

Note from Nancy

Stitch 'n Stretch is a unique elastic, consisting of a woven polyester band that has rows of spandex elastic cords running through it. You sew Stitch 'n Stretch to a flat garment along nonelastic guidelines that run the length of the band and then pull the spandex cords to stretch the elastic.

Joining Makes Label

I discovered a way to join the ends of sports elastic and identify each child's garment at the same time. I zigzag one end of the elastic to a piece of seam tape or nonraveling fabric, butt the other end of the elastic to the first end, and stitch it to the tape. The tape ends can be trimmed or tucked under the wrong side of the elastic. The tape helps my children easily tell front from back (I always position it at the center back), and each child's clothes are identified by a specific color tape.
Carol Brown, Bethlehem, PA
Another idea: *Alyce Eastman of San Diego, CA,* says it's easiest to use a large scrap of fabric or seam tape, trimming the excess after it's been sewn to the elastic. This flat application (as opposed to overlapping the elastic edges and sewing) means there's no lump where the elastic joins. She keeps fabric scraps with her elastics, always ready to use!

Quick Belts

To make an elasticized belt, I cut a piece of ¾"-wide (1.8-cm-wide) waistband elastic to equal the length I need and then cut a strip of fabric 2" (5 cm) wide and twice the length of the elastic. I fold the fabric in half lengthwise, with right sides together, and stitch a ¼" (6-mm) seam along the lengthwise edge. Then I turn the tube right side out and thread the elastic through the tube with a bodkin. Add a buckle and adjust the fullness, and my belt is done!
Delois Flage, Postville, IA
Another idea: *Darlene Hawkey-Cruikshank of Franklin, WI,* uses colored elastic without any fabric covering. She fastens the end of her elastic belt around a buckle using a 1½" (3.8-cm) length of Velcro hook-and-loop tape, which means she can use the same elastic with a variety of buckles to create different looks.

Gathering Stitch 'n Stretch

On my first two attempts to use Stitch 'n Stretch Elastic, I had a problem getting the gathers even on the end opposite that from which I was pulling the cords. On my third attempt, I stitched along the width of the casing in the center of the waistband and pulled the cords from both ends, gathering each toward the center. Success!
Lynn Carmouche, Huntington Beach, CA
Another idea: *Hazel Sepich, of Canton, IL,* uses a small dowel bought at a lumberyard to pull up rows of elastic evenly. For 1½"-wide (3.8-cm-wide) elastic, she cuts off a 2½"-long (6.3-cm-long) piece of dowel, puts a piece of double-faced tape on one side of the dowel, and wraps the elastic around the tape on the dowel. By turning the dowel, she pulls up the spandex cords. When she's through gathering, she sticks another piece of tape on the dowel over the length of elastic and cuts the elastic (or stitches across the end of the Stitch 'n Stretch before cutting the cords).

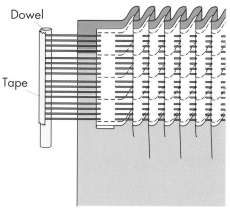

Pulling Elastic Cords

Lingerie Straps

I love to make lingerie and found a fun way of serging matching straps. I use ½"-wide (1.3-cm-wide) regular elastic (not lingerie elastic) and serge over the elastic with a 3-thread overlock stitch. I use woolly nylon thread and set my machine for a short stitch length. The straps fit snugly and never fall off my shoulders.
S.V., Boulder, CO

Sewn-In Garters

My daughter had trouble keeping her anklets from working down into her shoes until I zigzagged clear elastic (a transparent elastic that stretches to three times its original length) to the top of each sock just below where the cuff folds over. The clear elastic launders well, is not bulky, and helps the socks keep their shape. Since the elastic isn't visible when the socks are worn, you could use different thread colors to identify different children's socks.

Mary Lippe, Independence, MO

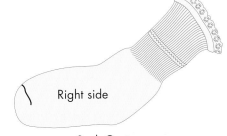

Right side

Sock Garters

Adjustable Stirrup Pants

When I drove while wearing stirrup pants, the pants pulled tight and were very uncomfortable, especially when I was driving a car with a standard transmission. Now I sew one end of Button-Up Elastic (elastic with buttonholes woven into the band) on one side of the pant bottom in place of the stirrup and put a button on the other side. I can either button the pants looser or unfasten the stirrups altogether while driving and then tighten or fasten them when I get out of my car.

Mae J. Cormier, Moncton, NB, Canada

Buttonhole Casing

Before making a casing for elastic, I make a buttonhole the width of the elastic (or slightly smaller) and about 1" (2.5 cm) from the side seam, toward the back. I then sew completely around the bottom of the casing, without leaving an opening on the bottom or in a seam for inserting the elastic. After the casing is completed, I insert the elastic through the buttonhole, including an inch or two of extra elastic for adjustments.

This is especially useful when I'm making garments for someone out of town—they can easily make size adjustments by pulling the elastic out through the finished opening, stitching it as tightly as they want it. The elastic slips back in neatly when the adjustment is complete, and no sewing is needed to close the opening.

Sue Nesmith, Monett, MO

Remove and Insert at Once

For years I've been replacing elastic in skirts and slacks, but only the other day did I think of pinning the end of the new piece to the end of the old one. As I pulled the old one out, the new one was inserted!

Margaret Higgins, London, OH

Buttoned-Up Sheets

I use Button-Up Elastic on the corners of fitted sheets that won't stay on the mattress. I sew a button about 7" (17.5 cm) away on one side of the corner and sew the buttonhole elastic about 7" (17.5 cm) away on the other side of the corner. Then I tighten the elastic to the desired snugness and button. Button-Up Elastic is easy to adjust and just as easy to undo to remove the sheet for laundering.

Debbie Schaefer, Brooksville, FL

ZIPPERS AND OTHER CLOSURES

From zippers and Velcro to drawstrings and hooks and eyes, learn to close any garment quicker, easier, and more securely.

Marking Fly-Front Zippers

When making slacks, shorts, or any garment with a fly-front zipper, I use the packaging from the zipper as a topstitching guide. The pattern calls for stitching 1½" (3.8 cm) from the center front, and that's exactly the measurement of this little guide. I store the guide in my sewing box.
Maraquita Steinmetz, DeLand, FL

Recycle Zippers

I've found that spray starch on a used zipper makes it easier to reapply to a new garment. Place the zipper on a flat surface (I use the top of my clothes dryer) and thoroughly wet the fabric with spray starch. Finger-press the sides to smooth the zipper and remove excess starch. Let the zipper dry thoroughly, and it's ready to reuse.
Virginia Leslie, Seburg, FL

Fuse a Zipper

By using fusible thread to position a zipper, I get my zipper to stay in place without using pins. Since fusible thread is too thick to go through my sewing machine needle, I fill a bobbin with it and stitch around the zipper with the wrong side up, making sure the fusible thread is on the right side of the zipper. After basting the seam in which the zipper will be inserted and pressing the seam open, I center the zipper on the seam allowance, press to secure it in place, and stitch with regular thread.
Marie Tartamella, Brackenridge, PA

Positioning Hooks and Eyes

Sometimes it's difficult to accurately stitch hooks and eyes to a garment because they tend to slip out of position. I temporarily attach them to the garment with transparent tape before I stitch. After sewing the hooks and eyes in place, I tear the tape away.
Bonnie Summers, Millstadt, IL

Alternate Eyes

When sewing metal hooks and eyes on waistbands, I found that the eye tended eventually to break the threads and pull loose. Now I use a safety pin in place of the metal eyes. And I found it's possible to make instant adjustments for changing waist measurements!
Coral Shinn, Medford, OR

Zippers in Fleece-Lined Jackets

When I tried to insert a new zipper into a fleece-lined jacket, I couldn't get both the lining and the outer fabric even. I fused the zipper to the lining with a strip of Stitch Witchery and then used the same process to hold the outer fabric in place. At last! The front and back edges met, and all I had to do was to sew a straight line!
Mary Ott, Livonia, MI

Marking Snaps

To line up the two halves of a row of snaps, I first sew all the ball portions of the snaps to the fabric. Then I rub chalk on each ball and press the fabric against the corresponding fabric piece. The chalk marks exactly where the sockets must be attached.
Jennie Joyner, Nashville, TN
Another idea: *Sarah Jepsen of Minden, NE,* uses the same basic approach to attach gripper snaps on children's clothing or Western wear. She sews on all the sockets first and then puts a piece of dressmaker's carbon paper between the layers of cloth. She taps the sockets with a hammer to make carbon rings where the studs need to be. The studs cover the rings and perfectly line up with the sockets.

Shortening Zippers with Interfacing

While sewing a knit top, I inserted a 22" (55-cm) zipper as the pattern recommended, but I didn't like the appearance. I decided to shorten the zipper to 7" (17.5 cm). First I bar-tacked a new zipper stop. Then I cut a small rectangle 1¼" (3.2 cm) long and the width of the zipper from fusible knit interfacing. Next I wrapped the rectangle around the zipper end sandwiching the zipper in the middle, and fused it to the end. This made a finish that's more comfortable to wear against my skin than a cut zipper end.
Julie Duffy, St. Petersburg, FL

Shortening a Zipper with an Eye

To shorten a zipper, I simply sew a flat eye from a hook-and-eye set across the teeth to make a new stop and cut off the excess length. *Josephine Matos, Bensalem, PA*

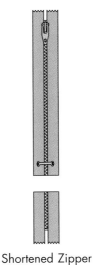

Shortened Zipper

Revive Drawstrings

The ends of drawstrings may fray during washings. When this happens, I trim each frayed end slightly, coat it with clear fingernail polish, and roll the coated end between my thumb and forefinger to make it look like the end of a shoelace. I let the drawstring dry, but halfway through the drying period, I roll the end a second time to compact and mold it. This works especially well on children's wear. *Dorothy Gilbertson, Elk Mound, WI*

Note from Nancy

Another way to coat the ends of the strings to prevent them from fraying is to use Fray Check seam sealant. Use this colorless liquid in much the same way described for using clear fingernail polish. Fray Check is completely washable and dry cleanable, too.

Velcro Sash Holder

To prevent a little girl's sash from sliding up and down on her dress, I place small dots of Velcro (loop side) in a few spots on the waist of the dress and then stitch corresponding dots of Velcro (hook side) on the sash. The sash always stays exactly where I want it.
Celeste Basil, Matteson, IL

Zippered Cosmetics Bag

Practice putting in a zipper with this supereasy cosmetics bag created from a ready-made quilted oval or rectangular place mat. When I find place mats in pretty colors on sale, I buy several to make into gifts.

Open a zipper. With the zipper and the place mat facing down, align one edge of the zipper tape along one short side of the place mat. Position the edge of the place mat next to the zipper teeth and stitch the zipper in place. Repeat to stitch the remaining short side of the place mat to the remaining edge of the zipper tape.

With the right side of the place mat on the inside and the zipper open, stitch the side seams from the ends of the zipper to the folded edge. (If you don't undo the zipper, you'll have no way to turn the finished product right side out!) If desired, miter the bottom corners to give the bag a base.

This makes a very quick-and-easy gift—even the seams are finished. When I give these away, I tuck little surprises inside. *Geri Pyrek, Horicon, WI*

NEEDLES AND PINS

You can't sew without needles and pins. "Sewing With Nancy" viewers help you size them, thread them, and keep up with them.

Sharpening Needles

To keep my sewing machine needles clean and sharp, I sewed a 2"-square (5-cm-square) pillow and filled it with an emery-like filling. (I used the filling from an old strawberry needle sharpener that comes on some tomato-shaped pin-cushions.) Before I thread my machine, I sew through the pillow.
Genevieve Paternek, Mountain Home, AR

Thimble Magnet

I bought a thimble with a recessed end, cut a magnet circle to fit, and glued the magnet in place. When I want to pick up a needle, I just hold my thimble over it. It's great!
Kathy Osborn, Memphis, TN

A Pin for Needles

I cut a 1½"-long (3.8-cm-long) magnetic strip and attached a craft pin to it by the magnetic force (you could glue it if you wanted to). Now when I'm hand-sewing, I pin the strip to my blouse, and when I'm not using the needle, I keep it safe and handy on the magnetic strip.
Margaret Medwick, Prescott, AZ

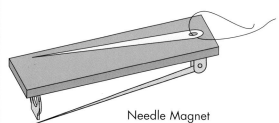
Needle Magnet

Another idea: *Ruth Boyd of North Powder, OR,* takes a similar approach to keeping needles handy. She applied a magnetic strip to the wall near her sewing machine and puts needles on the strip horizontally with larger needles near the bottom.

Reading Machine Needle Sizes

The other day I took the needle out of my sewing machine to insert a new one, and I couldn't read the size marked on the needle. I rubbed a washable black marker over the numbers and then wiped off most of the ink. Just enough ink remained in the numbers for me to read them with a magnifying glass.
Mamee McCarty, Lake Havasu City, AZ

Note from Nancy

Another way to read those tiny numbers is to use the plastic case in which the needle was packaged; the tops of many needle cases are magnified. To check the needle size, just place it into the case. Reading the number should be much simpler!

Finding the Hole

When changing the machine needle, I sometimes have a hard time locating the hole. I keep a small pocket mirror in my drawer and hold it under the shank to easily locate the hole in which to insert the new needle.
MaraLee Dyson, Iowa City, IA

Keep the Eye Straight

When inserting a new needle into my serger, I put a pin in the needle eye to keep the needle from twisting as I tighten the screw.
Rita Jacobson, Fountain Valley, CA

Easier Threading

I put a small piece of white paper behind my needle when threading it. It's easier to see the eye, and I can thread faster.
Charlotte Cain, Gasport, NY

Needle Chains

My 94-year-old mother-in-law still makes beautiful quilts, but she has trouble threading her needles. I thread 10 or 15 needles onto one thread (still on the spool) and put a quilter's knot at the end for her. She pulls the length of thread she needs through a needle, cuts the thread, and makes another knot. When she's used up all the thread on that needle, she simply repeats the process.
Joyce Grant, Salisbury, NC

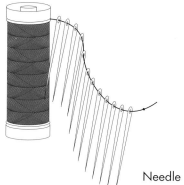
Needle Chain

Quilting Knots

I am making a Cathedral Windows coverlet, and it takes a lot of hand sewing. My needle kept unthreading, and I mentioned this to my husband. He sat quietly for a while and then handed me a threaded needle, and said, "Try this." It works great! He threaded the needle and placed a small knot at the base of the needle eye. The knot slips through the fabric just as if it weren't there.

He formed a thread loop and inserted that loop through the eye of the needle. Then all he had to do was put the needle point through the loop opening, pull, and he had a knot. That's all there is to it!

Mr. and Mrs. Robert Murray, West Lynn, OR

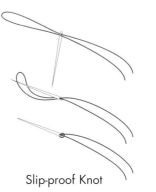

Slip-proof Knot

Using Clothespins for Pins

I buy miniature wooden clothespins at a craft store for ten cents each and use them for no-pins sewing. These clothespins have just enough pressure to clamp a seam allowance, holding two garment pieces together ready to be stitched. I can quickly pluck off the clothespins with my right hand as I sew, leaving the left side of the seam area flat and free for the other hand to guide the fabric along.

I use these little clothespins when regular pins might mar my fabric. Also, miniature clothespins are handy to clamp tissue pattern pieces together when I want them out on the sewing table for reference until my sewing project is complete.

Alice Colas, Meadville, PA

Putting a Lid on Used Needles

Since my sewing machine and serger get heavy use, I go through a lot of machine needles every week and also end up with (I hate to admit it) bent pins and hand needles. I used to worry about disposing of them in the regular trash: What if the bag broke on the way to the curb and someone stepped on a needle? A few times I stabbed myself on a discarded needle while retrieving something that fell into the wastepaper basket.

I didn't want this to happen to my two boys, who sometimes use the sewing room. Now I keep a 35-mm film canister on the sewing table between the sewing machine and the serger. I labeled it "used needles" and put a small hole in the lid so that I can drop in used pins and needles, like putting coins in a piggy bank. This way the lid never has to come off, and if the container tips over, the needles won't fall out. When the container is full, I cover the hole with tape, tape down the lid securely, and discard the needles safely, sealed in their container.

Arlene Paganucci, Sudbury, Ont., Canada

Free Clips

I have found that the plastic clips used by department stores to keep blouses and other garments folded are excellent for holding layers of leather, vinyl, or similar materials together when I don't want pinholes in the finished project. I often find these clips in fitting rooms, as well as on clothes I purchase. The clips are free and much less invasive than metal clips used for the same purpose.

Meng Wong,
Victoria, BC, Canada

OTHER NOTIONS

Notions can be homemade or purchased, and you can recycle sewing notions for nonsewing purposes.

A Disappearing Lesson

I often use disappearing-ink markers in my custom dressmaking business and tend to leave them lying everywhere—or at least I did until a customer picked one up and wrote a check with it. I noticed it only after she left. Since she lives four hours away, it meant having another check mailed to me. We had a good laugh over it, and now I put the pens away. (I also supply a four-year-old friend with these markers because she can't ruin her clothes or my walls with them!)
Darlene Dawling, Monterey, VA

Recycled Rotary Blades

I use my rotary cutter almost exclusively (instead of shears) to cut out patterns from fabric. The blades are expensive, and I don't want to throw them out when they're too dull for fabric. I put them in a special box, and when I use a new pattern (or draw corrections on waxed paper), I use the dull blades to cut out the paper pattern. It is so much faster than scissors, and I'm not throwing used blades away.
Lucile Atkins, Clanton, AL

Another idea: *Jacquelin Willmarth of Meadville, PA,* makes quick work of Christmas gift wrapping by using her old rotary cutter blades to cut wrapping paper. For gifts wrapped in the same size boxes, she cuts several sheets of paper at once. She's also used her rotary cutter and old blades to cut rough household items, including carpeting.

Note from Nancy

Another way to store these blades is in blade's original package. Label it "used blade," and when the blade becomes dull, return it to the package. Then it will be handy for cutting paper patterns, wallpaper, or other paper items.

Rubber Fingers

I cut the fingers off worn rubber gloves and wear the smaller pieces on my index and third fingers when I sew or quilt. I attach the largers ones to the points of my scissors with rubber bands before I store the scissors—they're great protection if I drop my scissors! Out of the palm and back area of the glove, I get eight or more needle pulls.
Madonna Breese, Clearwater, FL

Nonslip Rotary Cutting

No matter how carefully I held the ruler, my ruler always slipped as I pressed against it with the cutter and I ended up with crooked pieces of fabric. To keep the ruler from slipping, I took a round piece of rubber-like material used to open jar tops and cut the circle in half, giving me a straight edge. I put it under the ruler, and it works like a charm to keep the ruler from slipping as I cut.
Hilda Rosenzweig, Richmond, VA

Note from Nancy

Placing several Needle Grabbers rubber disks between the ruler and the fabric serves the same purpose. The Grabbers grip the ruler and prevent it from slipping.

Playful Help

My thread kept snarling when it unreeled from the horizontal thread spindles on my sewing machine. I needed a way to hold the thread vertical, so I raided my grandson's toy box and found some construction toys (such as Tinkertoys or Duplo Blocks). The toys were so easy to configure to change my thread feed from horizontal to vertical that I decided to try the same technique on my serger, this time going from vertical to horizontal. Next I tried it on my upright thread dispenser. All three applications worked very well for me.
Frances Smith, El Paso, TX

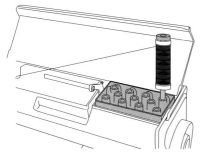

Thread Spindle

Get a Grip

I've used the Dritz Ezy-Hem Gauge for many years but had to be careful when pressing hems with it because it got so hot. Now I attach my quilter's tool handle to the gauge. It makes pressing the hem fast and easy, with no burned fingertips.

Florence Morgan, Polson, MT

Painted Machine Guides

To highlight the most used guidelines on my sewing machine throat plate, I've colored them in with permanent paint. (Hardware stores carry enamel paint in the form of a crayon.) You can also use permanent fabric paint, applying it with a toothpick.

Debra Meyers, Corvallis, OR

Another idea: Jane Bowers of Jackson, OH, color-codes her guidelines with fine-line permanent markers: red for the ⅝" (1.5-cm), blue for the ½" (1.3-cm), and green for the ¾" (1.8-cm) grooves. Just color a line, wipe off the excess ink with a tissue, and let dry before sewing.

Sewing Extrawide Seams

Because I leave extrawide seam allowances when I make slipcovers, I have found it necessary at times to serge off a wider strip of fabric than I have guide markings on my machine. One time I reached into the drawer for adhesive tape to mark a guideline and I pulled out buttonhole space tape by mistake. I realized it was perfect for adding extra guidelines to my serger and sewing machine. The tape has vertical 1" (2.5-cm) units brightly marked in ⅛" (3-mm) increments, and I can trim the tape to fit wherever I need it—to mark a stopping point to turn corners. Just trim, peel, and stick!

Peggy MacDonald, Riverview, NB, Canada

Rubber Band Gauge

As a substitute for magnetized seam guides, I place a wide rubber band snugly around the open arm of the sewing machine, located at the desired seam width. Fabric runs straight along the side of the band at the proper seam width.

Aleen Schiller, Tacoma, WA

Corner Guides

I use the markings on the throat plate to stitch even seams, but turning a square corner and stitching exactly ⅝" (1.5 cm) from the corner used to be trial and error. Recently I discovered that a sewing machine at my workplace had a marking exactly ⅝" (1.5 cm) in front of the needle. I went home and put a piece of tape on my machine to indicate the position ⅝" (1.5 cm) in front of the needle. Now I can turn the corner at exactly ⅝" (1.5 cm) with no guessing.

Laura Crawford, Tazewell, VA

Fray Check Dispenser

Here's a neat way to apply Fray Check liquid seam sealant: Clean a used-up nail polish bottle with remover and then fill the bottle with Fray Check. Fill a second cleaned bottle with alcohol to take care of mistakes. (If the nail polish bottle cover fits on the Fray Check bottle, clean only the cover/brush and screw it directly onto the Fray Check bottle.)

Aldine Macklem, Oakville, Ont., Canada;
Joyce Rose, Victoria, BC, Canada;
and Octova Roberts, Indianapolis, IN

Note from Nancy

Fray Check and other seam sealants dry out if the cap is not closed tightly. Make certain the cap is tight.

Custom Boxes

I sew for children and grandchildren out of town and cannot always find the right size box to ship finished items. Mailing envelopes can be costly, so I make my own by cutting four thicknesses of brown grocery bags to size and zigzagging three edges. I slide the item into the bag and sew up the other end. Presto! A double-thick mailing bag for free.

Anne Schwendeman, Baytown, TX

Note from Nancy

This is a great idea for packages sent via the U.S. Postal Service, but these mailing bags are not acceptable for UPS (United Parcel Service).

Parka Saver

I keep an Ezy-Pull Bodkin in my purse in winter to quickly restring parka hoods when dressing toddlers. It's also good if they pull out the string on car seat covers.
Tyral Craig,
Stamps, AR

Crochet Serger Tails

My serger is an invaluable addition to my sewing room, but I used to have a terrible time finishing off the serger tails at the ends of seams. It took me longer to thread the tails into a yarn needle to pull them back under the seam than I had spent serging the entire seam. "There must be a better way," I thought. Taking a small steel crochet hook, I ran the hook about 1½" (3.8 cm) under my serged seam between the thread and the fabric. I grabbed the tails with the hook turned toward the fabric (so that I wouldn't hook my serged thread), and easily pulled those tails through to secure them.
Ellen Faulkner, Magazine, AR

Other ideas: To pull serger tails underneath serged seams, *Jane Stewart of Mesquite, TX,* uses a dental floss threader. *Sharon LaMontagne of New Haven, MI,* suggests a knit fixer tool such as a Knit Picker. Two viewers—*C.T. of Carol Stream, IL, and Virginia Vining, of Cherokee Village, AR*— use narrow loop turners that are usually used for turning spaghetti straps.

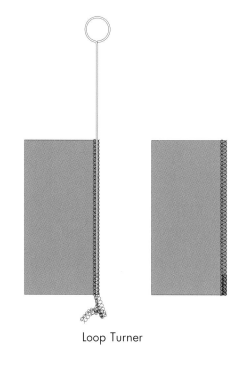

Loop Turner

Glued Tape Measure

I glued a tape measure on the edge of my sewing machine. It's always handy to measure things when I'm at the machine.
Dorothy Moreland, Ganzales, LA

Another idea: To avoid permanently applying a tape measure to her machine cabinet, *Audrey Roush of Cushing, WI,* uses Stikit Again & Again Glue temporary adhesive on the back side of a plastic tape measure. This lets her remove the tape measure without leaving a mark on the cabinet.

Guiding Yarn

While working on a quilt project, I decided to cover the gridding pencil marks by zigzagging 4-ply yarn over the top. I found it helpful to guide the yarn by threading it through a plastic straw cut in half on a diagonal. I hold the straw at a slant like a pencil, keeping the point at the bottom, directly under the toes of the presser foot. I can easily see where I'm stitching, and yarn fuzz doesn't get caught on the toes of my machine.
Frances Gilbert, Oceanside, CA

Tape Pull Tab

I like using transparent tape to mark zipper seams and other seam widths, and I find it easier to remove the tape (especially when it has been sewn through) if I prepare it first. I fold over ⅛" to ¼" (3 mm to 6 mm) on one end to make a pull tab and then press the tape to a scrap of fabric before applying it to the garment. The tape picks up a small amount of lint from the scrap, so it's less sticky but is still sticky enough to do the job.
Marge Jungnitsch, Grizzly Flats, CA

A Sharp Idea

The Gingher Sharpening Stone works on more than scissors or shears. It did a first-rate job sharpening my buttonhole cutter, making it as good as new.
Hilda Rosenzweig, Richmond, VA

Stronger Shower Curtains

The tops of shower curtain liners often tear before the curtain wears out. Sewing a strip of twill tape across the top (above the ring holes) makes the curtain last a lot longer! You could use bias tape or even a pretty ribbon on the right side of the curtain; fold under the outer edges to the first hole and then zigzag across.

Peggy Bonati, Republic, MO, and Anne Davis, Westminster, CO

Shower Curtain

Wearable Tape Measure

While sewing, I wear a tape measure around my neck like a necklace. In only a few seconds, I can use it to get an accurate measurement, which can save 15 minutes (or more) of ripping out an incorrect seam.

Marcia Mitchell, St. Joseph, MO

Easy Hem Gauge

When a pattern says, "Turn and press up ⅝" (1.5 cm)," it's hard for me to get a straight line. I cut cardboard strips in different widths so that all I have to do is fold the fabric over the correct width cardboard and press. I cut these strips with a craft knife or a paper cutter, and I reuse them, storing them near my ironing board so that they're handy when I press hem allowances.

Marilyn Dase, Sun City West, AZ, and Mary Bullock, Nobleton, Ont., Canada

Another idea: Strips cut from bleach jugs or other thin plastic items also make good seam gauges, according to *Coral Marbaugh of Van Wert, OH.* She writes sizes on hers with a permanent marker.

Instant High Chair Pad

When my granddaughter was old enough for a high chair, she was so small that she slipped down in spite of the safety strap. I had some Jiffy Grip (fabric with built-in grip backing) to make a seat grabber pad. To test the idea, I folded the fabric in fourths and put it on the seat—it worked perfectly! We're still using the folded material and will be able to use it for pajama feet when she's bigger.

Myrtle Giraudo, Elko, NV

Visible Bows

I have a four-year-old daughter who loves bows and barrettes. When faced with the dilemma of storing them, I came up with an easy solution. I cut a length of fabric seam binding (or bias tape or grosgrain ribbon) one yard long, folded it in half lengthwise, and made a loop at the top. Then I stitched across it at ½" (1.3-cm) intervals. The loop fits over a coat hanger, and the bows or barrettes are fastened to a section of the lower loops.

Janet Kear, Phoenix, AZ

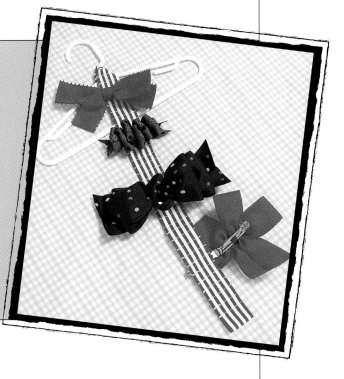

Sewing Machine Transportation

I take a lot of sewing classes and I have a heavy computerized sewing machine. A luggage rack helps me wheel the machine from the car to class. I can also stack my box of sewing notions (which is actually a tackle box) on top and strap it down. Then away I go!
Judy Greer, Lebanon, TN

Let There Be a Light Box

I have a Pfaff 7550 and a Sew Steady Portable Table. I keep a small fluorescent light under the large and convenient see-through table. It is the type of light you can readily purchase in a hardware store and has an off and on switch. When I want to trace a pattern, all I have to do is turn on the light, and—voilà—I have a light box. It is very convenient and works perfectly.
Justine Waller, Tucson, AZ

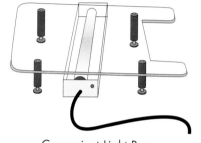

Convenient Light Box

Miniblind Seam Gauge

I made a hem/seam gauge that I find more convenient than the commercial markers that sometimes slip out of adjustment. I've also discovered the multimarkings on commercial gauges may be confusing to learning-disabled beginning sewers that I work with. I take discarded miniblinds slats and cut 6" (15.2-cm) strips. Then I mark one strip at ¼" (6 mm); a second at ½" (1.3 cm), another at ⅝" (1.6 cm). On the opposite end, I punch a hole so that I can hang the markers on my Peg-Board.
Loisteen Kearney, Lampasas, TX

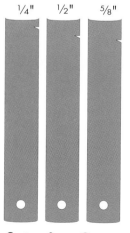

¼" ½" ⅝"

Custom Seam Gauges

It's A Wrap Up

If you want to keep extension cords, ropes, cording or rolled paper, such as wrapping paper, or pattern paper, from unrolling, use elastic scraps. Cut a length of elastic slightly smaller than the circumference of the item you want to secure. Almost any length and width of elastic over ½" (1.3 cm) works. Attach a snap or Velcro to fasten the two elastic ends together. Place the elastic around the item and fasten the closure; it will stay neatly in place.
Judy Mackey, Fort Worth, TX

Lengthening a Waistband Pattern

Here's a tip on lengthening a waistband pattern and keeping the notch marks in ratio to the extra added length. Mark the length of the waistband pattern onto elastic with a temporary marker. Also, mark notches, and center front. Place the lengthened waistband on the cutting board. Above the waistband, pin and stretch the elastic to meet the longer length. (The elastic will expand the marks in proportion.) Transfer the markings. For reduction, reverse the process. Mark the elastic the size of the smaller pattern. Stretch the elastic to meet the original pattern. Mark notches and other marks from the pattern. Relax the tension, and the notches are in proportion. Transfer all the markings to the smaller waistband.
Dorothy Benson, Prairie Village, KS

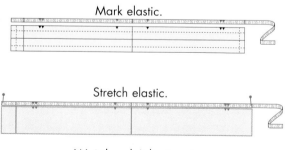

Mark elastic.

Stretch elastic.

Waistband Adjustments

Mat Grabber Organizer

I purchased two mat grabbers and I love them! They sure work well and keep my mats out of the way but handy. I hung them and my quilting rulers behind my laundry /sewing room door.

Diane Hafemeister, Cedarburg, WI

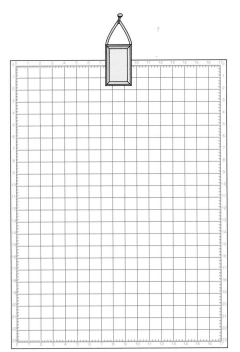

Hanging Mats

Rip to Recycle

I have found that a seam ripper is the best tool for removing labels from cans when I am preparing them for recycling. I also make "strip rugs" from polyester fabric, and I found that using zip-top plastic bags is a great help. You can divide up the various colors, put the fabric in the bags; then line them up to preview how the colors will look together. The same idea could be used for storing and organizing quilting scraps.

Arlene Beckman, Hannover, ND

Thread Substitute

One day when I was sewing, I ran out of white thread. I didn't want to stop everything, get dressed, and go shopping. Then I spotted my cone thread and knew I could do something. I took a craft stick, drilled holes on each end, and sanded the holes. I put one of the holes over the thread holder on top of my sewing machine and the other hole toward the back of the machine. I put the thread cone in back of the machine and threaded the end of the thread through the free hole on the craft stick. I continued threading the machine as usual. It worked great.

Annette Cepak, Arlington, TX

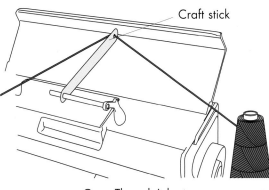

Craft stick

Cone Thread Adapter

Note from Nancy:

I like to use Annette's hint when I'm in a bind. But for regular sewing, I highly recommend using the stronger all-purpose sewing thread. Cone thread is only 2-ply compared to the 3-ply thread designed for sewing machines. (Seams sewn with 2-ply thread could easily pop in stress areas!) To add strength to seams sewn with cone thread, consider using two strands of cone thread instead of one.

No-Slip Hangers

I have a lot of Velcro hook tape left after doing crafts. Not wanting to throw it away, I found that I can take a 4" to 6" (10.2-cm to 15.2-cm) strip of the hook tape, fold it in half lengthwise, and glue it to a wire clothes hanger. It works great to keep wide-necked dresses and blouses from falling off the hanger!
Maxine Dunham, Edmond OK

Larger Fabric Tube

To make a fabric tube larger than can be accommodated by the Fasturn kit, find a heavy cardboard tube. Cut the length a bit shorter than the Fasturn turning wire. Thread the stitched fabric tube over the cardboard tube and proceed as usual.
Carolyn Czapor, Monroeville, PA

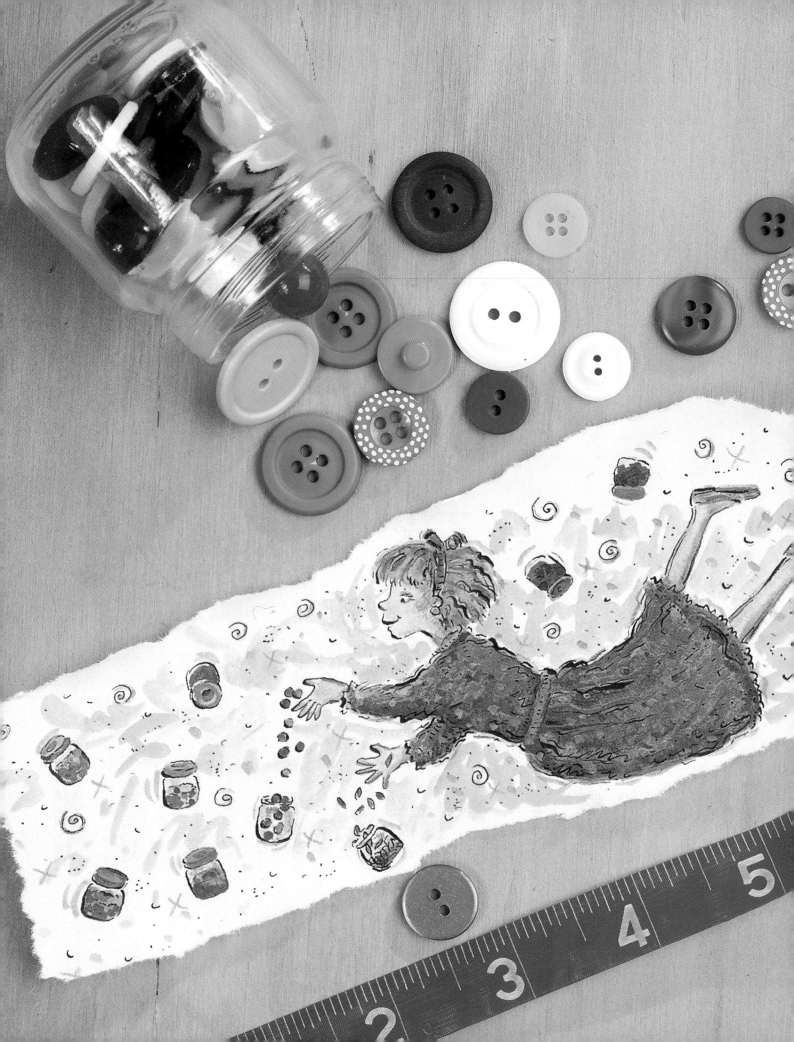

GETTING STARTED

Many of us think of sewing simply in terms of putting needle and thread to fabric. But there's so much more that has to be done before, during, and after the actual needle-and-thread part of sewing if we're going to create items that look professionally made:

• You must choose fabric, lay out the pattern, and mark the fabric pieces.

• If you're sewing clothes, you have to be sure that they fit the curves of your unique body.

• And while you're sewing, pressing correctly and at the right times can make the difference between a homemade-looking item and one that looks handcrafted.

You'll find a wealth of tips in this chapter to make all the basics faster and cheaper while still achieving professional results.

SPECIAL FABRICS

It's easy to fall in love with a particular fabric in the store, but successful sewing depends on matching the right fabric to the right project.

It's a Match!

As an admitted pattern hoarder and "fabrica-holic," I buy patterns and fabric I like, often without a plan for how to use them. When I'm ready to use a fabric that's been in my inventory for some time, I have to match it with a pattern that calls for no more than the amount of fabric in that piece. Two steps make this task easy.

First, when I get home with a new fabric purchase, I write the yardage and the width on a slip of paper and pin it to the fabric before I store it.

Second, when I buy a new pattern, I highlight the column listing the pattern size I'll be using and the yardage required. This helps me to be sure that I look at the correct size measurement and to easily determine whether I have enough of a particular fabric for that pattern.
June Boyle, Milwaukee, WI

Tissue Tips

When sewing a sheer fabric that tends to pucker, I place a 1½"- to 2"-wide (3.75-cm- to 5-cm-wide) strip of tissue paper under the fabric, covering the seam line. On some very sheer materials or laces, I use a strip of tissue paper on top also, sandwiching the seam allowance between the two layers of paper. I stitch the seams, using 12 to 15 stitches per inch to perforate the paper. I can easily tear off the paper, leaving a flat seam.

I have also used tissue paper while sewing satin to prevent making marks on the shiny surface when topstitching. And when I'm stitching across a previously sewn seam and want the bottom layer to remain flat while I stitch, I slip a piece of tissue paper under the material just as I get ready to cross the seam. This prevents the seam allowances from catching on the feed dogs.
Dixie Ehlers, Bedford, IA

Double Strength, Single Seam

Recently I worked on a project using marine-quality Naugahyde. I didn't want to depend on only one row of stitching; I also didn't want two rows of needle holes because I was afraid the holes would weaken the seam. I wound the bobbin with double strands of thread and used double threads through the needle (but only one needle). It reinforced the seam perfectly, and I had no trouble with the thread breaking.
Josephine Jackson, Meridian, MS

Soap Heavy Seams

When stitching heavy seams, I rub the seam allowance with a piece of bar soap. The sewing machine needle passes through the fabric with ease, and the needle doesn't break. This works great when sewing heavy denim.
Mary Louise Anderson, Mansfield, TX
Another idea: *Mrs. Louis Belotti of Roland, AR*, places a piece of waxed paper under the fabric to make it easier to slide the fabric under the sewing machine foot.

Making Insulated Fabric

If I want to make an insulated garment but can't find insulated fabric in the color or the design I want, I make my own by sandwiching a layer of fleece between two outer fabrics (or between an outer fabric and a lining). I stitch all three layers together around the outer edges and then treat them as one during construction. To keep seams of these several layers looking neat, I press the seams open and add a decorative stitch on the right side of the garment that straddles the seam.
Angela Wewel, Lakewood, CO

Pleats Show Grain Line

If I want to use fabric scraps left over after I've cut out a garment, I need to know the lengthwise grain of the fabric. Here's what I do:

First, I look at the weave of the fabric for threads arranged at right angles to each other. Along one of those thread lines, I fold a few pleats and hold them up to observe how they hang. Then I do the same thing on the other thread line.

One set of pleats appears rather stiff, but the other set hangs more gracefully. The set that hangs gracefully has the lengthwise threads running the length of the pleats, and I mark the lengthwise grain line with chalk for future reference.

Lengthwise threads are usually finer than crosswise threads. If texture or detail is added, it's usually added to a heavier or thicker crosswise yarn.

Lorraine Peterson, St. Petersburg, FL

Another idea: *Eva Stanley of Summerville, OR,* avoids trouble by marking the grain line on leftover fabric while it's still on the cutting table from the first garment. She uses a marking pencil or chalk, depending on the fabric color, and marks the grain line on the fabric's reverse side.

Tablecloths as Baby Bibs

The center of an old flannel-backed vinyl tablecloth is nearly always worn, but the edges that hang off the table are often like new. I use a bib pattern to cut out many baby bibs from these edges. Having flannel on the back is great because it prevents the bib from shifting, and the vinyl keeps food or drink from going through to the baby's clothes. These bibs make great gifts.

Carol Shashura, Beallsville, PA

Hand Towel Transformation

Hand towels seldom wear out as soon as their matching bath towels do. I use my mismatched hand towels as fabric for baby bibs. Sometimes I find that I can also use good (unworn) portions of bath towels to make these useful bibs.

Fern Groman, Seattle, WA

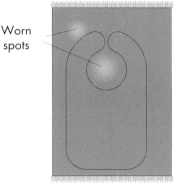

Worn spots

Hand Towel Bib

Linens Become Layette

Before the word *recycle* entered my vocabulary, my mother taught me to see pieces of fabric in different modes. She told me how her mother made bridesmaid dresses from linen tablecloths in London, England, and how wonderful the fabric was. My mother made robes out of chenille bedspreads and elegant children's coats out of ladies' coats.

As my first grandchild was about to arrive, I used the old fabric from my daughter's recently redecorated bedroom to outfit the bassinet and to make nursery items. The bassinet ruffle was originally a dust ruffle on a twin-size bed, and the matching bed sheets became a pillow, a quilt, and flat and fitted crib sheets. I also made a pouch with ribbons to tie on the bassinet; inside the pouch I placed a small album with the history of how the set was made, leaving room for pictures of all the little babies who will enjoy the bed.

Sally Mundinger, West Bend, WI

Note from Nancy

To test shrinkage and color change in washable silk, first make a control sample by cutting two 4" (10 cm) squares of fabric. Wash one square in cool water and leave the other square as a control sample. After washing, set the iron on the wool setting and iron the square until dry.

Compare this square to the control square. To prewash a large piece of silk, soak it in the bathtub and press to dry. NOTE: Don't be surprised if the water turns the color of the fabric.

Sewing Silk's a Dream

When working with lingerie or slippery fabric, place an old pillowcase (the older the better) over the arm of the sewing machine cabinet and secure the pillowcase with tape. It helps to keep the fabric from sliding off.
Rena Wehling, Brookfield, WI, and Bertha Crowder, Red Oak, OK

Skidproof Satin Sewing

I put a piece of nonskid fabric (like the kind used on the bottom of pajama feet) under and to the left of the sewing machine or the serger to keep slippery fabrics from sliding off the sewing surface. It works great for sewing evening gowns, bridal attire, or lingerie.
Lois Tumbleson, St. Petersburg, FL

Spray Satin

When I sew on slippery satin-type fabrics, I use a glue stick or a pattern spray (such as Pattern-Sta) to match seam allowances and secure hems. I don't have to worry about my fabric sliding out of place.
Kayla Zimmer, Loveland, CO

Note from Nancy

Glue or Pattern-Sta can also be used to secure the pattern to the fabric, eliminating the indentations and irregular edges that sometimes result when pins are used. In addition, pinholes often don't disappear from satiny fabrics. However, when using glue, remember it's only necessary to use a tiny dab.

Sewing Silkies Without Static

For sewing washable silky fabrics, I mix one part Perfect Sew stabilizer with two parts water and use that solution to make the fabric more manageable. For two yards (1.8 m) of fabric, I use about one cup (236.8 ml) of solution, putting it in a spray bottle and wetting the fabric completely. Using a spray bottle reduces waste since I only spray as much as I need. If I have time, I let the fabric dry until it no longer feels sticky; if I'm in a hurry, I speed the drying by using a hair dryer. When the garment is finished, I rinse it twice in lukewarm water. The results are wonderful! Since I've been using this method, I enjoy working on silky fabric and there's no static cling.
Earline Jensen, Lynn, MA
Other ideas: *Adele Corke of London, Ont., Canada,* uses a strip of Seams Great under each seam of silky fabric to prevent "pokies" (raveled threads) from showing through her seams. *Helen F. Warner of Williamstown, WV,* binds all the edges of a garment with fusible interfacing when sewing fabric that ravels.

Stable Knit Edges

When making a cardigan from knit fabric, I usually finish the neck and front edges with a band of crosswise grained fabric. I interface the band with fusible tricot, using the crosswise grain stretch on the area that will go around the neck and the straight grain down the front. This allows me to stretch the band somewhat at the neck for better fitting and to keep the front stabilized for buttons and buttonholes.
Ev Tamminga, Randolph, WI
Another idea: *Denese Klco of Mentor, OH,* stabilizes crosswise grained seams (shoulder seams or bias-cut seams) on knits by serging clear elastic (1-to-1 ratio) into the seam. Denese uses $\frac{1}{4}$"-wide (6-mm-wide) elastic or cuts $\frac{3}{8}$"-wide (1-cm-wide) or $\frac{1}{2}$"-wide (1.3-cm-wide) elastic in half lengthwise. This gives a nonbulky, firm seam with great elasticity.

Note from Nancy

Most knits used for dressmaking fall into one of two types: an interlock knit or a jersey knit. Each has particular characteristics.

An **interlock** knit is a type of double knit, which means it looks the same on both sides of the fabric. You may use either side of the fabric when constructing a garment. When you stretch an interlock knit on the crosswise grain, it remains relatively flat and smooth and doesn't roll.

A **jersey** knit is a single knit, which means each side of the fabric has a distinct appearance. There is a right side and a wrong side, and the two cannot be used interchangeably. When a jersey knit is stretched on the crosswise grain, it rolls toward the right side of the fabric. If a jersey knit is heavy enough, this rolling isn't a concern. But with a lightweight jersey knit, rolling sometimes makes it difficult to accurately stitch the narrow $\frac{1}{4}$" (6-mm) seam allowances shown on many patterns designed especially for knits.

Hemming Denim

If you hem jeans by double-folding the fabric for the hem (fold the raw edge in by half of the hem allowance and then fold again), the thickness of the side seams can be very hard to stitch through. When you turn up the hem allowance, clip up to the new hem fold line on each side of the leg seams and cut out a notch containing the bulky seam allowance. Then stitch the hem in place. Now you stitch through only two thicknesses of the leg seam rather than the three that would have been there without the notches. Those days of breaking needles when hemming jeans are over, and the jeans don't ravel in that area.
Janet Reichelderfer, Circleville, OH, and Joyce Day, North Liberty, IN

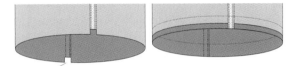

Notch   Double-Folded Hem

Another idea: *Janet Klaer of Stamford, CT,* makes seams in denim and other thick fabrics go through her machine easier by placing a rolled-up scrap of fabric under the back side of the presser foot when she reaches a thick seam. This levels the foot and enables her to sew more easily over the bulk—plus the machine doesn't skip stitches.

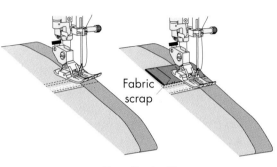

Fabric scrap

Easy Denim Hem

Don't Serge Velcro

Caution: Do not serge over Velcro. It not only broke my loopers, but also affected the timing of my machine.
Lois Tumbleson,
St. Petersburg, FL

Recycled Jeans Apron

One morning my husband asked if I could make an apron for him to wear in his garden. After looking through my fabric scraps, I decided nothing was suitable. Then I got the idea of using his old jeans.

I cut out the back of the jeans, including the pockets and 5" to 6" (12.7 cm to 15.2 cm) below the pockets. I opened the center back seam and overlapped the pieces to straighten the seam and to form a flat section. Then I hemmed the side edges.

I cut out the front of the jeans, including the zipper, the waistband, and the pockets. I opened the center seam below the zipper, straightened the pieces as for the back, and then hemmed the side and lower edges.

I placed the back section under the front section and topstitched the two pieces together.

Using parts from the pant legs, I made straps for the neck and the waistline and topstitched them in place.
Mary Cormack, Bracebridge, Ont., Canada

LAYOUT AND MARKING

A little extra care in laying out a pattern can make sewing faster. A disappearing-ink marker, chalk, and even your iron can make marking so much easier!

Matching with Pins

When matching plaids for sewing, I place the pins in alternating directions. This seems to prevent the seam from shifting, which would result in a mismatched plaid. I've used this method even with a very small (1/4" or 6-mm) plaid, and the results were just terrific!
Theresa Gajewski, Livonia, MI

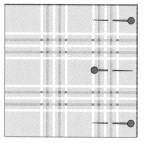

Matching Plaids

Tablecloth as Cutting Aid

I purchased a piece of oilcloth fabric with a 1" (2.5 cm) square pattern and then numbered squares from 1 to 36. Now I can measure fabric for yardage and get a straight grain at the same time. It also helps me lay out patterns on the straight grain and provides a good work surface.
Christine Lindenstruth, Pewaukee, WI

Preview Your Project

Some of my friends quit sewing because they couldn't tell what a particular garment would look like until they had finished it. Then they often didn't like the end result and wouldn't wear the garment.

To help me picture blouses, vests, and children's clothes, I fold a large piece of paper in half and place a pattern piece on the fold. Then I trace and cut out the pattern piece, leaving the outer portion of the paper intact to become a viewing pattern. I place the unfolded viewing pattern on a fabric, moving it around to various parts of the fabric design to see the effect. If I don't like what I see, I haven't wasted the fabric. Better yet, I can take the viewing pattern to the store with me and test it on a variety of bolts before making my purchase.
Geraldine Dempsay, Williamsburg, KS

A Chilly Hint

Have you ever used an air-soluble marker to transfer pattern markings and then found that you didn't have time to complete the project right away? To keep the marks from disappearing, I put the item in a zip-top plastic bag and place the bag in the refrigerator. The marks remain for six or seven days, depending on how dark the marks were originally.
Gayle Domorsky, Flint, MI

Pattern Saver

Before pinning a pattern to fabric, I place a piece of transparent tape at each spot I'm going to pin. This way, each time I use the pattern, I know where to place the pins in order to get the fewest puckers in the fabric. Frosted tape works well because it doesn't yellow with age like cellophane tape does.
Sue Hastings, Puyallup, WA

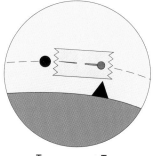

Transparent Tape

Note from Nancy

Placing tape on frequently used patterns also prevents tearing holes in the patterns. Sewer's Fix-It Tape works great for reinforcing the pinning locations.

A Dot Marks the Piece

When I'm making a pattern that includes several different views, I mark dots on the pattern guide sheet near all the instructions that apply to the particular view I'm making. This helps me quickly identify which steps I need to complete.

Also, if a pattern piece has more than one cutting line (such as for various sizes), I use a tracing wheel and tracing paper to mark the cutting line I need directly onto the fabric. This saves the pattern piece for future use and is especially helpful with multisized patterns for a growing child!
Anna Griesacker, Stafford, VA

Double-duty Pattern Paper
I save the backing from peel-and-stick vinyl shelf covering because it has dots marked ½" (1.25 cm) apart and makes great pattern paper. It's smooth and well marked.
Betty Tiffin, Riviera, AZ

Sharp Chalk
To keep a sharp edge on marking chalk, I put the chalk edge into the notched part of a plastic tag that comes on bread or produce bags. All I have to do is pull the plastic tag across the edge I want to sharpen. This method gives me good control, little waste, and a uniform edge.
Barbara Meyers, Bolingbrook, IL

No-Mark Grain Lines
Instead of extending a short pattern grain line marking with a pen or a pencil, I simply fold the pattern piece back along the grain line. This gives me a much clearer view of the fabric and its grain line, as well as a longer grain line to measure.
Rita Taylor, Oswego, KS

Quick Grain Line Finder
I use a clear 6" x 24" (15.2 cm x 61 cm) quilter's ruler for lining up the pattern grain line with my fabric grain line. The ruler works great when I'm using 45"-wide (114.3-cm-wide) fabric, folded in half. I can easily look through the ruler and see the arrow on the pattern. No more measuring and remeasuring!
Jean Thirud, Sidney, MT

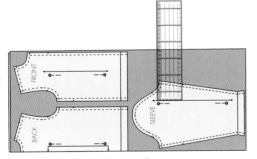

Quilter's Ruler

Weigh Patterns Down
For inexpensive, attractive fabric weights, I fill empty, washed baby food jars with sand, small pebbles, aquarium gravel, dried beans or grains, or glass marbles. Then I spray-paint the lids and put them back on the jars. I glue a circle of felt or fine-grain sandpaper to the jar bottoms so that they don't slip.
Cynthia S. Engel, Friend, NE

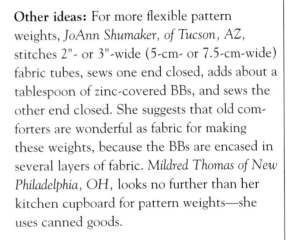

Other ideas: For more flexible pattern weights, *JoAnn Shumaker, of Tucson, AZ*, stitches 2"- or 3"-wide (5-cm- or 7.5-cm-wide) fabric tubes, sews one end closed, adds about a tablespoon of zinc-covered BBs, and sews the other end closed. She suggests that old comforters are wonderful as fabric for making these weights, because the BBs are encased in several layers of fabric. *Mildred Thomas of New Philadelphia, OH*, looks no further than her kitchen cupboard for pattern weights—she uses canned goods.

Note from Nancy
Using canned goods can be a convenient alternative to using pattern weights. Before securing the pattern with weights, I recommend pinning the grain line of pattern pieces parallel to the selvage. Then use weights to secure remaining edges. This technique works especially well on large pattern pieces.

A Weighty Gift
My pattern weights are ordinary creek rocks that have been hand-painted— a gift from my 13-year-old granddaughter for Christmas 1973.
Dorothy Suter, McMechen, WV

A Movable Stash

Each time we move, my husband looks at my fabric stash and says, "That stuff has to go! I'm not moving it again!" Much to his surprise (and chagrin), it shows up in our next home—I use it to cushion and wrap fragile items and to fill not-quite-full boxes so that they stack properly. And there's no useless paper to throw away!

Kitty Kontak,
Lake Jackson, TX

An Easy Match

On some patterns, each notch is marked with a number, and the numbers of notches on corresponding pattern pieces are the same (for example, a "2" in the shoulder seam allowance of the front pattern matches a "2" in the back pattern). When cutting out a pattern, I use a water-soluble marker to write the appropriate number for each notch in the fabric seam allowance. Then I match numbers when sewing pieces together. This is especially helpful for new sewers or for veteran sewers working on a garment with complex construction.
Sunny Greenwood, Orange, CA

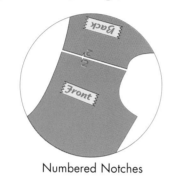

Numbered Notches

Another idea: *Clare Mosher of Prescott, AZ,* doesn't stop at marking notches on her fabric pieces; she puts a strip of masking tape on each fabric piece as she cuts it out, noting which piece it is. This simplifies assembly.

Sewing Machine as Marker

I was preparing a slim pull-on elasticized waist skirt pattern, and I needed to add ¼" (6 mm) to each side seam for more ease. Instead of measuring and marking the addition on the front and back pattern pieces with a ruler and a pencil, I took the thread out of my sewing machine and "sewed" my pattern pieces ¼" (6 mm) from the pattern cutting line. It was very easy to cut my enlarged pattern along the needle perforations.
Lois Miskoe, Rocky River, OH

Quick Light Table

Make a temporary light box for tracing designs and patterns by placing a lamp (without the shade) under a glass-top table. The glass provides a perfect surface for tracing. If you don't have a glass-top table, use a dining or kitchen table with a sliding leaf mechanism. Slide the table open, place a piece of glass or Plexiglas in the opening, put the lamp underneath, and trace. It's much easier and more accurate than trying to trace while standing at a sunlit window.
*Dorothy Mitten, Apache Junction, AZ;
Marg Gagnon, Gloucester, Ont., Canada; and
Judy Lilly, Daniels, WV*

Self-lined Knit Skirt

In the past I avoided buying T-shirt-weight knit fabric to make tops and matching skirts because I found the knit just too light for a satisfactory skirt. The hems of lightweight knit skirts (especially single knits) rarely have enough weight to hang properly.

My solution: For each skirt, I start with a tube of fabric twice the length of the finished skirt plus two waistline casing allowances. For a full skirt, I use a 60"-wide (152.4-cm-wide) knit tube, which eliminates the side seams. For a narrower skirt (hip size plus 2" or 5.1 cm), I make a tube by sewing one or two long side seams. For either style, I meet the cut edges with wrong sides together, so that the bottom fold becomes the hem and the skirt is self-lined. I finish the top with a casing and flat nonroll elastic or with a stitched-in elastic treatment such as Stitch 'n Stretch. I particularly like this technique for light-colored summer skirts because the self-lining eliminates the need for a slip.
Barbara Emodi, Halifax, NS, Canada

Press for Success

When using multisized patterns, I cut out the largest size and then press the pattern pieces along the cutting lines to use a smaller size. On necklines, armholes, and other areas where the cutting lines are curved, I clip the tissue so that I can press under the edges to use one of the smaller sizes. I can reuse the larger size simply by repressing, eliminating the need to cut separate paper patterns for the larger sizes.
Florence Salotto, Philadelphia, PA

Note from Nancy
This is especially helpful when you're sewing for growing children, where you know you will need a larger pattern size eventually.

Other ideas: *Michele Doerflein of Memphis, TN,* highlights the cutting lines for her size on a multisized pattern before she begins cutting. *Valerie Voigt of Detroit Lakes, MN* sometimes uses different colors of tissue paper to cut different sizes from a multisized pattern. Valerie stores her one-size tissue patterns in the original pattern envelope, writing on the back of the pattern envelope which color tissue corresponds to each pattern size.

Disappearing Marks

I use a disappearing marker to check off instructions on sewing patterns after I've completed them so that I know where I am at a glance.
Ann Perry, Myrtle Beach, SC

Save Your Patterns!

I purchased two sizes of paper hole punches to correspond to the large and small dot sizes found on patterns. I reinforce the dots with transparent tape and then punch through the pattern dots. This creates holes for inserting a marking pen or a chalk tip or for making tailor's tacks. The dot holes don't grow to tear up my pattern pieces as happened when I pinned, cut, or edge-clipped to mark my patterns.
Rita Taylor, Oswego, KS
Other ideas: *Betty Scott of Towson, MD,* places a strip of pattern tracing material (such as Do-Sew) over the pattern before she traces darts and other marks, reusing the same strips of pattern tracing material for several patterns. *Jennifer Diggs of Raleigh, NC,* puts strips of Sewer's Fix-It Tape over sections where she'll be using a tracing wheel (such as darts and pleats). *Eleanor M. Zic of McKeesport, PA,* reinforces her entire pattern by fusing waxed paper to the back of the pattern pieces.

Red Means Stop

A small step saves me much aggravation: I use pins with red heads as signals to stop, such as at the exact point of a dart or at the end of a zipper allowance or other point where I will need to change stitch length. If I'm using pins without colored heads (i.e., silk pins), I simply put two pins right next to each other.
Betty Naugle, Saratoga, CA

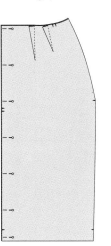

Stopping Point

Easy Does It
Do you sometimes start a sewing project but stop in midstream because you get tired of the project or can't quite figure out how to proceed? One of my sewing secrets is selecting an easy pattern. Then I don't get frustrated!
Melanie Miller, Madison, WI

Note from Nancy
At age 12, Melanie entered a vest and culottes in the "Sewing With Nancy" Challenge contest. Her garment placed first in the Junior Creative Designs Division.

Mark with Soap
Since dust from chalk bothers my allergies, I save slivers of soap to mark fabric. The soap comes off easily.
Jacquelin Mintal, Chicago, IL

Note from Nancy
Avoid using colored or perfumed soaps because they may leave residue.

FITTING

Every person has a unique set of body curves that a sewer must accommodate to get a custom-tailored fit—and children need growing room as well.

Sew the Curves

The teacher of a tailoring class I attended many years ago said that since females have curved—not angular—bodies, we should sew darts with a slight curve rather than making them perfectly straight.
Rose Marc-Aurele, Brick, NJ

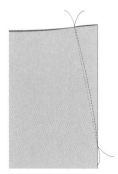

Stitched Curved Dart

Copier Pattern Enlarging

I had a problem finding one pattern with a large enough size range to make a set of matching dresses for my daughters (ages four and one). I finally purchased a pattern with infant sizes small through extra large and cut it even larger for my four-year-old. I used a copier to enlarge pattern pieces small enough to fit on the copier glass. I experimented to find the correct enlargement amount (15% for my child). After that I simply had to be sure any markings remained the same distance from the raw edges as they were on the original pattern piece.
Betsy Lowery, Helena, AL

Fitting a Big Bust

Since I am *very* well endowed in the bust and hollow chested above, I make my bust alteration by pivoting from the armhole notch instead of from the shoulder seam, as suggested in most fitting books. This results in a much smoother fit in the shoulder and chest areas while still allowing plenty of room for my bust. Of course, it opens the side dart considerably, but with the pivot-and-slide method, I don't have the problem of distortion from the slash-and-spread method I'd used before.
Nancy Wherry, San Diego, CA

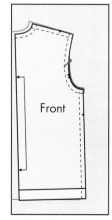

Front

Bust Alteration

No-Hem Pants

My petite two-year-old girl's pants are often too long for her. I rip out part of the hem on the inseam of each leg, run elastic through the hem to fit her ankle, and resew the hem. (I rip out the inseam because I don't always have thread that matches exactly and the inseam doesn't show as much as the outer seam.) The elastic holds the pant legs tight so that they don't drag on the floor. As she grows, I take out the elastic, and I don't have creases or lines that hems would make (which means she can wear her pants longer). I've used this method on both regular pant legs and snap legs and also on one-piece sunsuits when the legs seemed too wide and too long.
Audrey Steider, Geneva, NE

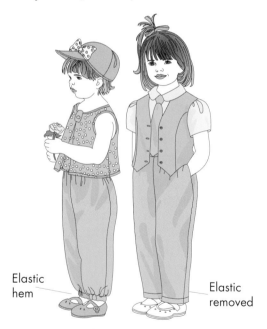

Elastic hem

Elastic removed

Elastic in Hem

Belt Your Dress Form

I sewed a band of 2"-wide (5-cm-wide) elastic that is 1" (2.5 cm) shorter than my waist measurement and slipped it over the waist on my dress form. When I cut pattern pieces for a skirt, I pin them to the elastic after taking in any pleats and darts. I also use the elastic band when fitting a bodice. I pin the darts on the bodice and then pin the bodice waistline to the elastic.
Rachel Rondeau, West Warwick, RI
Another idea: *Cora Williams of Elmer, NJ,* notes that it's much easier to put on and to remove garments from a dress form (especially knit garments) if you first slip a plastic bag from the dry cleaners over the dress form.

Thrift Store Patterns

I have scoliosis (a back curve), which makes it difficult for me to fit clothes from a standard pattern. I shop in thrift stores until I find a garment that fits me right off the rack. I buy it (often for less than I would pay for a pattern), wash it, and then cut it in half, exactly down the middle of the back. I take half the garment carefully apart, press it, and use it as a pattern to cut out another garment. I use the remaining half to figure out the construction sequence.
Margaret Hooker, Dallas, TX

Long-distance Fitting

I sew for people of a variety of ages and sizes, male and female, who live far away. To make fitting them easier, I cut the "How to Measure" section from a mail order catalog and tacked it to the bulletin board in my sewing room. The measurement charts come in a variety of sizes (from Infants to Women's Half Sizes and more), and the measurements coincide with the measurements used by the various pattern companies, right down to hem lengths (very helpful when sewing for children). I ask each person I sew for what size he or she wears, and then I can simply compare that size to the charts on my wall to determine the appropriate measurements.
Linda Bergstrom, Othello, WA

Slippery Hips

It's fun to make overblouses and tunics, but I've always hated the way they got hung up in back (on my generous hips) every time I bent a little. Now I use Wonder-Under to fuse a lightweight piece of silky lining fabric where my figure is fullest, and this eliminates the problem. My tunic skims my slacks as if I were wearing a slip. It also works great for maternity smocks.
Patricia Longerot, Albuquerque, NM

Tunic Lining

Embellished Hem Extenders

To allow for growth when making a little girl's dress or skirt, I provide a generous hem and add piping or lace at the hemline. When I let down the hem, the piping provides an attractive accent with no faded or worn line from the original hem to reveal that the garment has grown with its wearer.
Cindy Dworetsky, Englewood, CO
Another idea: *Yvonne Ragan of Seattle, WA,* always puts in at least a 4" (10.2-cm) hem, and when a still wearable dress becomes too short, she machine-stitches ¼" (6 mm) from the hem edge to create a tuck. Then she takes out the hem, presses the tuck down toward the bottom of the dress, and sews a narrower hem, disguising the wear-line with the tuck.

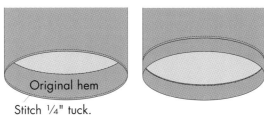

Stitch ¼" tuck.

Hidden Hem Lines

Picture This!

I love making clothes for my granddaughter, but she lives many miles from me. My clever daughter-in-law placed a large piece of paper on the floor and had my granddaughter lie down on it. My daughter-in-law then traced her body and made a chart of all my granddaughter's measurements. Now every garment is a perfect fit.
Peg Groh,
Clearwater, FL

Expandable Waist

I sew buttons on skirt waistbands with elastic thread. The band can expand with me after I've eaten a little too much dinner!
Ruth Doll,
Walnutport, PA

Sew Ribbing Flat

When I put ribbing on the sleeves and the legs of infants' and children's clothing, I put the ribbing on flat before stitching the leg or sleeve seams. To keep the edges of the ribbing even and to prevent slipping, I put a dab of fabric glue inside the ribbing fold on each side and also between the two seam edges. I let the glue dry a few minutes before serging or sewing the seams. The ribbing will not slip, and the edges remain even.
Eva Selnick, Cypress, CA

A Measuring Trick

I measure my children for pattern sizing using the centimeter side of my tape measure. This keeps my 10-year-old son from sucking in his stomach until the measurement is 22", which is the waist size he thinks he should have. He has no preconceived notion of a "correct" size when I use centimeters, and the finished garment fits perfectly.
Beryl Leonard, Seattle, WA

Note from Nancy

If you normally use the metric system for measurements, reverse Beryl's instructions, using the inch side of the tape measure. This idea can work with adults, too. After all, we probably have a pretty accurate idea of how big 38" or 40" is, but we probably don't know exactly what 96.5 cm or 101.6 cm means.

Center Extension

Our grandson has a very long torso, making him too long for one size yet too small for the next. I found that I could cut the too-short garment in half at the waist and insert a strip of rib knit the length needed to make the garment fit. This works on jumpsuits, bubble suits, and any other one-piece clothing. I have used both matching and contrasting rib knit. This saves a lot of money for us, because we don't have to go to the next size until his body grows overall.
Pat Aymond, Deville, LA

Note from Nancy

A child's pattern size doesn't necessarily correspond to the child's age. To determine a child's size, measure the child's width—chest, waist, and hip. Then determine the length, waist to floor and neck to waist. A child often grows taller much faster than his or her circumference measurements change. Many times it's possible to use a smaller size pattern that corresponds to the widths and then merely add length as the child gets taller.

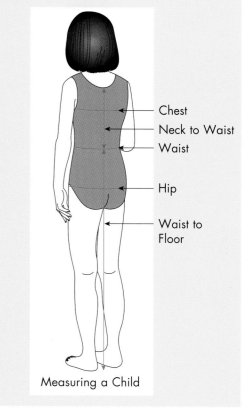

Chest
Neck to Waist
Waist

Hip

Waist to Floor

Measuring a Child

Temporary Waist Fitting

I find the 1½"-wide (3.8-cm-wide) size of Stitch 'n Stretch Elastic great for growing-room adjustments in the fitted waistband of ready-to-wear pants for growing children. I usually buy pants a little large (for longer wearing time), and that usually means the waist has a bit of extra room and may gap. To temporarily fit my son's waist, I stitch a piece of Stitch 'n Stretch across the inside back of the waistband (or I use two sections of elastic if the waistband has belt loops). My son tries on the pants, I adjust the elastic cords until the waistband gap closes, and then I satin-stitch the elastic in place. The waist now has elastic across the back.

The pants stay up with no gap, are comfortable to wear, and still appear neat from the right side. As his waist expands, I can snip, loosen, or resew the elastic cords until the waistband is finally left flat. This allows an extra season or two of wear!
Carol Ragin, Philadelphia, PA

Another idea: Buttons and buttonholes are the solution *Chris Elkins of Kansas City, MO,* uses to fit her children's waistbands. Chris stitches very flat buttons to the inside waistband of pants and sews several buttonholes at ½" (1.3 cm) intervals along a strip of elastic. She stitches one end of the elastic to the side of the waistband and can tighten or loosen the waistband as the child grows. She can remove the elastic strips when her child finally outgrows the pants and reuse the elastic in other clothes.

Note from Nancy

Stitch buttonholes vertically to prevent stitches from popping. Horizontally stitched buttonholes could lose shape.

A Children's Time Limit

When sewing for children, I never cut out more than I can sew during a week (or a month, at most). Children grow so fast! If I delay sewing a cutout garment for a few months, chances are it will no longer fit.
Sandy Halpin, Lynchburg, VA

Superquick Child's Swimwear Cover-up

I made a quick swimsuit cover-up for my daughter from a standard cotton bath towel. I chose cotton for its absorbency and its ability to breathe in our scorching summer weather.

I folded the towel in half lengthwise and cut a neck opening in the center that is several inches larger than my child's head. I folded 3"-wide (7.6-cm-wide) ribbing in half and sewed it to the neck opening using a ½" (1.3-cm) seam allowance. This resulted in a 1" (2.5-cm) crew-style collar. Then I added 12" (30.5-cm) lengths of ribbon (four ribbons, two on each side) for ties at the waist and applied a purchased appliqué that I found at the bottom of my sewing basket. Voilà! An adorable cover-up that doubles as a towel!

From start to finish, I spent 15 minutes on the project. Because it is so sturdy and not fitted, my daughter will wear it for several summers, but I look forward to making more of them—the possibilities of color combinations and embellishments are endless.
Linda Evans, Chandler, AZ

PRESSING

Get dimpleless darts and sharp creases every time by using these easy hints.

Sharper Pleats

For sharp pleats or creases without stitching, lay a strand of ThreadFuse along the inside of a pleat or a crease and press to fuse.
Sharon Britton, Thornton, CO, and Helen Rawls, Bossier City, LA

Preheat Iron Water

Because I hate to wait for water in an iron to get hot, I heat the water for the iron in a small pitcher in the microwave. It's easy to fill the iron using the pitcher, and I have instant steam. I also heat my spray bottle of water in the microwave because warm water soaks into garments much faster than cool or room temperature water.
Nellie Pierce, Casa Grande, AZ

Tie Pattern Pieces Down

To prevent pattern pieces from blowing off my ironing board, I put a wide piece of elastic around the end of the ironing board and pin the ends together. When I'm finished with a pattern piece, I tuck it under the elastic to secure the pattern.
Lorraine Laufenberg, Pittsburgh, PA

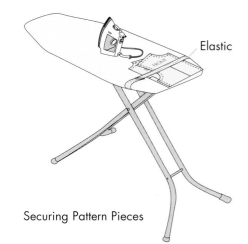

Elastic

Securing Pattern Pieces

Note from Nancy

The elastic band also works well to keep pens and pencils from rolling off the ironing board, as well as to keep shears from accidentally being knocked off the board.

Ironing Cord Tieback

I sewed a large drapery ring onto the end of my ironing board to run the iron cord through. This prevents the cord from sliding around the side of the ironing board and causing wrinkles when I press fabric or large projects.
Laura Brown, Hebron, OH

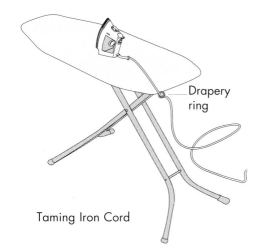

Drapery ring

Taming Iron Cord

An Oversize Ironing Board

I took a ceiling panel such as those used in suspended ceilings, covered it with several layers of batting, and then covered the entire thing with a sheet. I folded the ends of the sheet under and stapled them to the bottom, but you could make a casing for a drawstring to hold the cover taut. I now have a 24" x 48" (61 cm x 121.9 cm) ironing board that is light to store and works fine on a table or a kitchen bar or across the top of a washer and a dryer. It's great for pressing curtains or my husband's pants.
Zellah Lamoreaux, Marissa, IL

No More Up and Down

When I make a garment, I sew in one sitting as many seams as possible that don't intersect each other. Then I press all these seams at once. That way I don't have to get up and down as often.
Tyral Craig, Stamps, AR

Time It

I usually cut out several garments at once so that I can save time fusing interfacings. I line them up on my ironing board and use an electric timer, setting the number of seconds needed for fusing each piece. When the bell rings, I lift my iron with one hand and reposition it to the next location, resetting the timer with my other hand. This way I'm not guessing at the number of seconds needed, getting impatient while counting, or losing count if I'm interrupted.
Margaret Ragland, Madras, OR

Sponge Replaces Press Cloth

I've just started quilting and naturally want all the pieces and the seams to be ironed just right. Unfortunately I can't steam using a press cloth, because I can't see what I'm doing. Therefore I had trouble getting the quilt as crease free as I'd like.

I took a new sponge and cut a piece about 1" (2.5 cm) wide off the end. I keep the piece on the end of my ironing board, along with a small cup of water. Now all I have to do is saturate the sponge with water and wipe it over the crease with one hand while I iron the crease with the other. I can iron anything crease free in no time at all and be able to see what I'm doing.
Margaret Schwartz, Anaheim, CA

Vinegar Sets Creases

I use a solution of one part vinegar and eight parts water (¼ cup or 59.2 ml vinegar and 2 cups or 473.6 ml water) to take wrinkles out of fabric and to put creases in. I put the solution in a spray bottle, label it, and keep it with my iron.
Doris Brandhof, Hampstead, NC

Automatic Moistener

I put a clean, wet sponge in a plastic bag and place my press cloth in the bag after each use. The press cloth picks up moisture from the sponge and is just damp enough for the next round of pressing.
Genevieve Paternek, Mountain Home, AR

Tear-Away Press Cloth

I put a small piece of loop Velcro on one corner of my press cloth and the hook piece on the wide end of my ironing board so that the press cloth is always right where I need it. Having the soft (loop) side of the Velcro on the press cloth prevents the cloth from grabbing or clinging to what I'm pressing.
Darlene Jurgenson, Clarkfield, MN

Easy Permanent Creases

A close look at my husband's finer ready-to-wear pants showed they had a strip of glue holding the creases. To get the same effect, I put fusible thread in the bobbin and water-soluble basting thread on top of the machine. While the pant leg is still flat, I stitch along the crease line, with the right side of the fabric up. Then I fold the pant leg, wrong sides together, along the stitching line and press. The fusible thread melts, securing the crease. To remove the basting thread, I lightly spritz the crease with water.
Roseann Hutchins, Redlands, CA

Easier Pant Pressing

When pressing pant creases, I find that it's much easier if I turn the ironing board around. This puts the pant waist at the wide end of the ironing board, which supports the body of my pants better than the tapered end and makes it easier to press.
Kathy Steinhauser, Fairview, PA

Creasing Polyester

To get a really sharp, permanent crease on polyester, I first press the crease with a damp press cloth (before I sew the garment) and then immediately replace the damp cloth with a piece of wool fabric. I press until dry with the iron set on "wool." Believe it or not, it works!
Lois Smith, Pueblo, CO

Perfect French Seams

I sew baptismal gowns and party dresses for children. My French seams sometimes would pucker or ripple even though I pressed them when I was finished. Then I discovered what I was doing wrong: I waited to press the seams until they were complete. I now press both sides of a seam after the first stitching, stitch the second time, and then press again. The seam turns out beautifully (and it makes the second stitching easier to do).
Kathleen Choren, Milwaukee, WI

Finding Time to Sew

Lack of time is my biggest problem. I know that most of you share my sentiments. I do try to sew in small segments of time. (Remember, I wrote the book 10-20-30 Minutes to Sew!) Regardless, I still struggle with sewing time taking away from my family time. My preschooler, Tom, insists on sewing with me; he's my sewing room companion. At first I wasn't too keen on this two-person operation because it wasn't too productive, but now it's become a fun time together. I keep a box of fabric scraps, glue, and paper for him to create with while I cut out patterns, fuse interfacing, etc. Once I'm at the machine, he's a "Lap Lander," pulling out pins as I come to them and clipping threads at the end of a seam. I'm fortunate to have a desk in my sewing area, so my almost-teenager, Ted, does his homework while Tom and I are the tandem sewers. When I make my sewing time somewhat family time, I find more time to sew without neglecting the kids. Now...if I could just get my husband to cut out patterns instead of "channel-surfing"!

Pressing Ultrasuede

I've enjoyed working with Ultrasuede for many years and use a press cloth to prevent the steam holes on my iron from leaving marks. However I've found that rubbing a scrap of Ultrasuede over the pressed area renews and lifts the nap. Also, when I'm only fusing (not stitching) an Ultrasuede appliqué in place, I spritz the bonding agent on the wrong side of the appliqué before positioning it. Steam doesn't readily penetrate Ultrasuede, so spritzing from the bottom creates steam to form a better bond.

Rita Thomsen, Davenport, IA

More Kitchen Sewing Aids

Many home sewers have discovered freezer paper's many uses in sewing but may not know that parchment paper is another wonderful addition to any sewing room. I use it like a Teflon pressing sheet for fusible interfacing or Wonder-Under—nothing sticks to it, so it protects the ironing board cover. I use a second piece as a press cloth, and I use it over and over. Parchment paper is available on a roll, like waxed paper, at larger grocery stores and at cooking stores.

Judy Worrell, Watertown, WI

Pad Alters Interfacing

I had difficulty properly fusing interfacing until I realized that the problem was my foam rubber ironing board pad. It was just too soft to make a good pressure contact. I purchased a new pad (the old-fashioned felt type) and—presto!—no more problems.

Marilyn Hoffman, Oconomowoc, WI

Dimpleless Darts

I learned how to press darts properly in a tailoring course. I cut the dart open almost to the end and then place a threaded needle in the lower, uncut point of the dart before final pressing. This keeps the uncut dart end from flattening out. I cut a small circle of fusible interfacing and fuse it over the dart point on the wrong side of the fabric. No dimples! The reason I use a threaded needle is so that I can pull out the needle by the thread tails after pressing and avoid getting my hands close to the hot iron or the heated needle.

Pat McGovern, Roselle Park, NJ

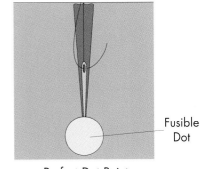

Fusible Dot

Perfect Dot Point

Prepress Hems

While my fabric pieces are still flat, I prepress any hems. After the garment has been sewn together, it's much easier to touch up a prepressed hem with an iron before hand- or machine-stitching. I especially like to do this on smaller areas, such as sleeves, where pressing after assembly can be difficult. Always determine the exact hemline length before pressing—if there's any doubt about the hem length, wait until you're certain before pressing.

Kristine Marsh, Tucson, AZ

Do I Need Floss, Too?

When teaching beginning sewing classes, I tell students that an important tool for pressing is an old, clean toothbrush and a cup of water. When I need a little extra moisture in a particular area, I use the toothbrush to dab on a small amount of water before pressing. This seems to help when using a household iron that doesn't produce quite enough steam.
Gayle Domorsky, Flint, MI

BASIC SEWING TECHNIQUES

It's easy to take the basics of sewing for granted. After all, we know how to stitch a straight seam and hem a dress.

Yet small changes in the way you accomplish such everyday sewing jobs as gathering a skirt waist or fusing interfacing can make big changes in the time required and the quality of your results. Saving just a few seconds each time you stitch a straight seam would eventually add up to hours that you could spend sewing more projects. A quick-and-easy change in the way you attach collars could greatly improve the quality of your finished garment.

Take advantage of the hundreds of years' worth of combined sewing experience that the "Sewing With Nancy" viewers offer in this chapter's hints. You'll find some new ways to complete sewing basics.

SEAMS

Whether you're stitching them, reinforcing them, or taking them out, seams are the backbone of every sewing project.

Quick Geometry

To make an easy 45° corner for shaping the ends of waistbands, tabs, pocket flaps, and such, I simply fold any straight-edged paper so that two adjacent edges meet. This forms a 45° angle that I can pin to my fabric.
Lucile M. Olson, Traverse City, MI

Never-Ending Basting Thread

It always seemed that just when I got into the rhythm of long, easy basting stitches I had to stop and rethread the needle. I ended this problem by threading my needle but not cutting the thread until I finish stitching. Now I only have to rethread if I run out of thread on the spool.
Frances Mabry, Karnes City, TX

Glue Seams in Place

I use Liquid Pins to glue down seams that are going to be joined to another garment section (for example, skirts to waistbands or sleeves to bodices) so that they don't shift or fold in the wrong direction while I'm stitching. (I also use this technique to keep seam allowances in place when I sew quilt sections.)
Rachel Levitan, Rochester, NY

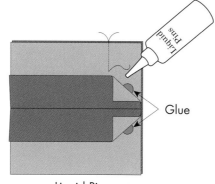

Liquid Pins

Staple Seam Allowances

When using a serger, I found pinning—even parallel to the edge—to be a nuisance, since stopping to remove pins defeats the speed feature of serging. My solution is to match the seams and to staple the fabric pieces together in the seam allowance. The staples hold the fabric perfectly, and the serger knife safely and neatly cuts off the stapled fabric. This requires a heavy-duty stapler when working with heavier fabrics.
Eleanor Taylor, Westbrook, ME

No More Thread Anger

A scrap of fabric saves me a lot of "thread anger"—frustration over having to rethread my needle, watching my thread bunch under the throat plate, or wasting thread with long thread tails in between seams. At the end of a seam, after I backstitch as usual to secure the seam end, I simply sew across this scrap of fabric and then cut the threads between the scrap and project, leaving the needle in the middle of the fabric scrap until I'm ready to start the next seam.
Millie Zlesak, Black River Falls, WI

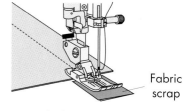

Fabric scrap

Smooth Threads

Another idea: *Elizabeth Zwicke of Waukegan, IL,* uses a 3" x 6" (7.6-cm x 15.2-cm) piece of Stitch-N-Tear as a starter cloth. She slips the Stitch-N-Tear scrap under the edge of any lightweight fabric that might be forced down into the throat plate.

A Beautiful Hint

I purchase extralong manicure sticks from a beauty supply store (you might be able to obtain one from a manicurist) and use them to ease fabric under the needle. The sticks are lightweight, and the 6" (15.2-cm) length is a comfortable size to handle.
Doris Brewer, Edneyville, NC

Reinforcing Skirt Vents

To prevent a skirt vent from tearing, I reinforce the top of the vent with the straight eye from a hook-and-eye set.
Teresa Gaddes, Charlotte, NC

Self-Binding Fabric

After cutting out a garment, I cut narrow strips along the selvage and use these strips in place of seam binding to reinforce seams at both the shoulder and the waistline. This way, I'm always assured of a perfect color match.
Baben J. Patricelli, Garden City, SC

Note from Nancy

This great hint is especially applicable when sewing knits. Many times I suggest using Stay-Tape as a stabilizer in the shoulder seam. Using the self-fabric selvage edge is a thrifty alternative.

Making Points

I use a typewriter eraser (the kind that comes in pencil form) when turning collars, cuffs, or other items with corners. I have a little pencil sharpener in my sewing box so that I can keep a decent point on the eraser. I can push the point of the eraser into the corner without worrying that it will make a hole. I shorten the stitch length for about 1" (2.5 cm) on each side of the point to reinforce the seam.
Dorothy Abben, Largo, FL

Removing Threads

Rather than pick out all the individual threads after I rip out a seam, I lay a strip of masking tape along the seam, press firmly, and then pull off the tape. The tape pulls out all the cut threads, leaving a clean sewing area without harming the fabric.
Jeanne Vital, West Covina, CA

Paper Corners

When sewing a sharp corner, I avoid a fabric jam by tucking a small piece of paper under the corner as I approach it. The paper gives me something to hold onto after I have pivoted and am ready to stitch the next side of my square. The paper then tears away easily and can be placed under the next corner. I also use this technique when topstitching or sewing patch pockets, or any time I'm sewing a very narrow seam allowance.
Merry May, Tuckahoe, NJ

Let the Machine Do the Work

When serging two uneven lengths, I always sew with the shorter length on the top and the longer length on the bottom. The under layer eases in as I serge. This is especially helpful when I'm setting in a sleeve with some ease and when I'm applying ribbing or elastic.
Naomi Baker, Springfield, OR

Note from Nancy

Naomi is the author of numerous books on serging and sewing. Whenever Naomi gives me a hint, I pay attention!

Seams Like a Great Pillow

Too thrifty to toss out the legs my daughter cuts off pairs of jeans to make shorts, I sew the bottom of a cutoff pant leg, stuff it with foam or fiberfill, and then stitch the top closed. For some pillows, I add lace and ribbon trims. The denim pillows are so popular in my daughter's college dorm that many of her friends have asked me to convert their cutoff jeans legs into pillows! *Juanita Coleman, Bedford Heights, OH*

Note from Nancy

What a great way to recycle those extra denim pieces! Here's a jeans pillow variation that saves even more time. After a pant leg is cut off, hem the cut end. Insert foam or fiberfill and then secure both ends with rubber bands. Cover the rubber bands with ribbon ties. The ties and the bands can easily be removed when the pillow needs to be washed.

Starching Knits

The cut edges of T-shirt, single, or jersey knits don't roll while I sew if I first spray them with starch and then lightly press.
Esther Stepke,
Milwaukee, WI

Improve Your Grades

I've always disliked grading seam allowances because it's time-consuming, and my seams often end up looking dreadful. Many times I've snipped into wrong parts of the seam, the garment, or my fingers. Out of desperation I tried using my rotary cutter and mat; to my amazement I had neat seams in a fraction of the time, with no wrong snips. I cut one seam allowance the desired amount and then flip the garment over to cut the other seam allowance. On straight seams, I use a clear plastic ruler, making it even faster and more accurate.
Carlene Maurer, San Jose, CA

Note from Nancy

When cutting small curves and around small pattern pieces, be sure to use the regular-sized rotary cutter rather than a larger cutter. The smaller blade is easier to navigate in curved areas.

Easy Tube Turning

When making straps or apron ties, I fold the fabric with right sides together and then place a piece of silky seam binding along the fold on the inside, next to the right side of the fabric. As I stitch one end and the side seam, I catch the seam binding in the end seam and use it to turn the tube inside out. The seam binding ravels easily if I need to keep the end seam, but if both ends of the tubes should be open, I simply trim the end seam. This works as well as a purchased metal tube turner.
Mary Atkins, Richmond, VA

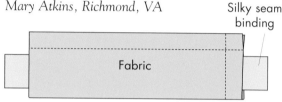

Silky seam binding

Fabric

Tube Turner

Making Dark Seams Visible

While ripping out seams to alter a navy blazer, I had trouble seeing the dark thread against the dark fabric. I rubbed tailor's chalk over the seams and was pleased to see that the stitches stood out, making it easy to use my seam ripper. I'm sure this would work as well on any other dark color fabric and thread.
Patsy Arcement, Marrero, LA

A Soapy Solution

I place thin pieces of soap (too thin to use at shower time but too much to throw away) in a terry bath mitt made from a hand towel.

After folding back 1" (2.5-cm) hems on both ends of the towel, I stitch ¾" (1.9 cm) from the folded hems to form casings. Then I fold the towel in half, with wrong sides out (meeting the casings), and stitch the sides together up to the casings. I cut wide elastic to fit my wrist and insert the elastic into the casings.

I put pieces of soap into the mitt to use in the shower. The mitt prevents the wet soap pieces from slipping out of my hand.
Geraldine Hooker, Dallas, TX

No-Sew Seam Closing

Instead of hand-sewing closed the seam opening in a pillow or other object that's been stuffed, I use fusible web. I fuse a piece of web as wide as the seam allowance and as long as the opening onto the right (not wrong) side of the seam allowance in the area of the opening. After I turn the project right side out and stuff it, I peel off the paper and fuse the opening closed. This leaves a clean finish that is quick and unnoticeable.

Donna Yukim, Iron River, Alta., Canada

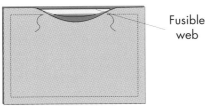

Closing Seams

Stretch Stabilizer

While sorting laundry I noticed that elastic had been used as a stabilizer on the shoulder seams of one of my husband's knit shirts. Since I've never liked the idea of making stretchy knit fabric unstretchy by using twill tape to stabilize the seams, I duplicated this ready-to-wear technique, using ¼" (6-mm) clear elastic as a stabilizer. Now I have a seam that gives when it needs to but keeps its shape.

Deanna Wheeler, Lebanon, MO

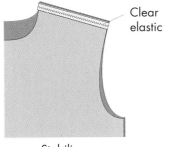

Stabilizer

Another idea: After cutting scraps of fusible hem tape in half lengthwise, *Susan La Rose of Knoxville, TN*, irons the scraps to the wrong side of stitched shoulder seams in interlock knit blouses.

Easy Snipping

When clipping close to a stitching line (such as into a V neck or when fitting a curved piece to a straight piece), I have often either snipped right through the seam or have failed to come close enough to the stitching line. Using a buttonhole cutter (blade and block) instead of scissors keeps that from happening. I just position one corner of the blade next to the stitching line and rock the blade back and forth. I can see exactly how close I am to the stitching line because I'm working from the inside out. (This also works well when stitching and trimming scallops.)

Barbara Minor, Pocatello, ID

Buttonhole Cutter

Note from Nancy

A number of viewers wrote to tell me that they reinforce the area of the fabric to be clipped by fusing a small patch of lightweight iron-on interfacing to the wrong side of the fabric before cutting.

Reversing Serger Seams

I found it extremely difficult to remove serger stitching until I figured out how to effectively use my seam ripper. I insert the tip of the ripper between the two pieces of fabric and under the stitching that wraps around the seam. I carefully rip through the entire length of the seam and can then easily pick the stitches. The needle thread comes off in one long piece, and I remove the short pieces with a lint brush.

Ellen Taylor, Johnsonburg, PA

Threadless Stitching

I'm nine years old and learned to sew just a short time ago. So that I could practice sewing straight, my mother took the thread out of our sewing machine, and I sewed over straight lines drawn on a piece of typing paper using an unthreaded needle.

Anita Schwebach, Dumont, MN

Note from Nancy

It's easier to feed paper through the machine than to feed fabric, and it gives a beginning sewer a feel for how to guide fabric and use the machine. As a gift idea, try decorating plain paper by stitching with a decorative stitch to create personalized notepaper and greeting cards.

GATHERS, PLEATS, AND SEAMS

Viewers share their ways to make gathering quick and easy, to get crisp pleats, to sew whiskerless French seams, and so much more.

Wrap Thread for Darts

To keep the sewing machine threads taut when I sew straight darts, I put a pin crosswise at the dart point/dot and wrap the thread tail around the head of the pin.
Nancy Pappenfuss, Pleasanton, TX

Better Gathering Control

When I use a double row of stitching to create gathers, I stitch the first row of gathers on the seam line. Then I pivot and take two stitches toward the edge of the fabric; I pivot again and stitch the second gathering row parallel to the first row. When I pull the threads to gather my fabric, the pivoted stitches control the threads at the end opposite the one I'm pulling, so I don't have to worry about pulling out the threads.
Melba Crowder, Lawrenceburg, TN

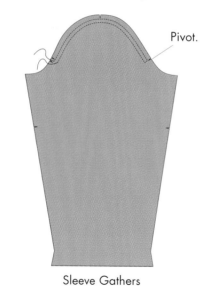

Sleeve Gathers

Use Cording Foot to Gather

When gathering fabric or veiling, I place pearl cotton or narrow cord along the seam to be gathered and then use a cording foot and a large zigzag stitch to sew over the cotton or the cord. The edge is simple to gather by pulling the cotton or the cord.
Amy Williams, Janesville, WI

Double Needles Speed Gathering

When making gathered curtains, don't take the time to sew two rows of gathering stitches. Instead use a double needle and a long basting stitch to sew along the edge to be gathered. For most applications, pull up the bobbin thread; for gathers across very small areas, pull up the two rows of double-needle stitching.
Sarah L. Kingsbury, Warren, OH, and Diana Graham, McLoud, OK

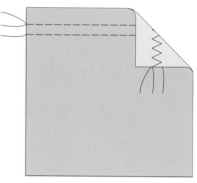

Gathering with Double Needles

Step by Step

Many dress patterns suggest completing the bodice, completing and gathering the skirt, and then attaching the skirt to the bodice. When sewing for my preschool-aged grand-daughters, I've found that it's easier to attach the front dress bodice to the gathered front skirt and then separately attach both back bodice pieces to the gathered back skirt. Then I sew the shoulders and insert the sleeves, finishing the dress by sewing each sleeve and side seam in one long seam.
Mary Needham, Plainville, CT

Grading Gathers

After sewing ruffles to flat fabric, I trim half the ruffle seam allowance but retain the entire seam allowance on the flat fabric. I fold the flat seam allowance over the ruffle seam allowance and zigzag it in place within the seam allowance, using a wide zigzag stitch and making sure the zig goes over the raw edge. I think this looks neater than simply zigzagging over the raw edges. This technique also works when stitching together many layers of fabric—I simply trim all except one layer, wrap the untrimmed layer over the trimmed layers, and stitch.
Patty Richeson, Dunnigan, CA

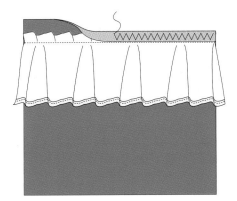

Finished Seam Allowance

Gathering Lace by the Yard

When my daughter was married two years ago, she chose a wedding gown pattern and a bridesmaid dress pattern that each had yards and yards of ruffles—the bridal gown alone had 40 yards (36.56 m) of gathered lace—and I don't have a ruffler for my machine. Then I remembered that when I use the longest stitch on my machine, the fabric usually puckers. So I purposely set my machine at the longest stitch and tightened the upper tension to get the lace as ruffled as I wanted it. As I sewed, I adjusted the tension to get the gathering just right. I left long thread tails on each strip so that I could make changes when I sewed the completed ruffle onto a gown. Using this technique, I finished the dresses ahead of schedule!
Sandi Roe, Dunedin, FL

Tape Pieces Together

When attaching a ruffled fabric piece to a flat piece, I hold the ruffles together with ⅛" (3-mm) double-stick basting tape. The tape keeps the ruffles from being smashed down or pushed out and is especially helpful if you don't have a walking foot for your machine.
Lexi Reynolds, Neenah, WI

Smooth Ruffles

Recently I was making a quilt for my first grandchild and wanted to add a gathered ruffle around the quilt. To make a 2"-wide (5.1-cm-wide) ruffle, I folded a 4"-wide (10.2-cm-wide) strip of fabric in half lengthwise, meeting cut edges, and serged the cut edges together with a rolled edge. I inserted a double needle into my sewing machine and threaded crochet thread through the hole in the throat plate. By stitching ⅝" to ¾" (1.6 cm to 1.9 cm) from the serged edge along the length of the ruffle strip, I encased the crochet thread. To gather the ruffle, all I did was pull the crochet thread.
Louise Moody, Newalla, OK

Fishing for Gathers

To gather a large area, I zigzag over fine fishing line. The fishing line is easy to draw up, won't break, and is quick to remove once I've attached the gathered piece. Fishing line works on both light- and heavyweight fabrics.
Marj Reth, Independence, IA

Combine Machines

To gather material, I first serge the edge to be gathered. Then I stitch over the serged stitches using a conventional machine set at basting, leaving long thread tails to pull the gathering threads. The serging helps the fabric lie flat so that the edges won't curl, and it gives a clean finish.
Tammy Maddock, Flint, MI

Gather with Elastic

I use clear elastic to gather fabric, and it works beautifully! I cut the elastic 1½" to 2" (3.8 cm to 5.1 cm) shorter than the length to be gathered (such as a waistband), divide both the elastic and the garment waistband into quarters, and then match quarters. When I stretch the elastic to meet the fabric and zigzag over it, I get instant, even gathers. This makes skirt-making a little faster!
Laura Adams,
Gallatin, TN

Sew Flat Ultrasuede Seams

Flatlocking (a serger stitch option) is a great way to seam Ultrasuede. I set my needle tension a little tighter than for a normal flatlock so that when the seam is pulled flat, one side overlaps the other. This results in a seam that is similar to a lapped seam, but with a great stitching accent. Flattening the seam takes a little practice, but one side naturally wants to overlap the other. I place my thumbs on either side of the seam and wiggle the seam back and forth to straighten it.
JoAnne Stingl, Greenfield, WI

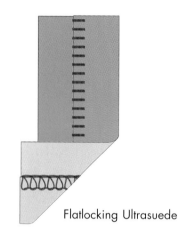

Flatlocking Ultrasuede

Whiskerless French Seams

I like to use French seams for underarm and sleeve seams in dressy blouses, but French seams can be time-consuming to stitch, trim, and stitch again. And if I'm not careful, I have trouble with whiskers from the encased seam allowance, especially with fabrics that tend to ravel. I now do the first stitching with a serger set on the narrowest setting (2.5). This trims the whiskers and encases the seam allowances. Then it's easy to press, fold, and prepare for the final stitching.
Linda Boelter, Rhinelander, WI

Tucked Inserts

I pleated fabric to make a collar without having to stitch all the tucks. Instead I pressed the tucks and then applied fusible interfacing to the back of the pleated fabric before I cut out the collar.
Susanne R. DeLeon, Miami, FL

Frozen Pleats

Freezer paper makes sewing pressed or unpressed pleats so much more accurate and quicker for me.

I trace the pattern section with pleats onto freezer paper (the kind with a wax coating on the back) and cut it out. Then I use either a pencil or a tracing wheel to transfer the pleat lines onto the freezer paper. With a warm iron, I press the paper onto the fabric, positioning the paper just below the top seam line.

I fold the paper-backed fabric along the pleat lines and press. Then I stitch along the seam line and stitch again about ¼" (6 mm) above the seam line to stabilize the seam. When I peel the paper away from the fabric (it comes off easily), I have perfect pleats every time!
Caroline Winter, Rochester, MN

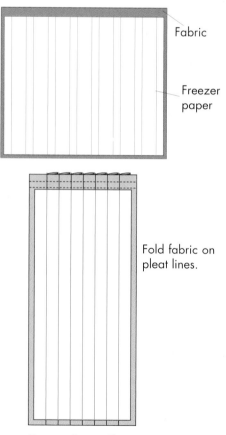

Fabric

Freezer paper

Fold fabric on pleat lines.

Freezer Paper Pleats

Pintucked Pleats

My daughter wanted a pleated skirt made from fabric so wrinkle-proof that I couldn't press pleats with anything resembling a knife edge. Enter the pintuck foot and the edge guide! I used a double needle and the pintuck foot to make a series of tucks on the right side of the fabric, turned the fabric inside out, and did the same thing on the wrong side. Presto! I had permanent pleats.

Evelyn McKinley, Kent, WA

Note from Nancy

Generally the hem is one of the last sewing steps, but when making a pleated skirt, hem the skirt and then stitch the pleats. This change of sewing order will give a very professional look.

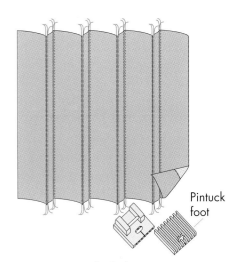

Pintuck foot

Pintucked Pleats

Color-code Pleats

When marking pleated skirts, I use one color of chalk to mark the fold lines and another color for the lines to which I'm folding. This is easier for me to see than large and small dots.
Arlene Oettmeier,
Bay City, MI

A Traveler's Needle Case and Pincushion

One of my favorite gifts to give is a small needle case and pin holder—friends who travel love it. The needle case requires two small ready-made doilies about 4" (10.2 cm) in diameter, three pieces of felt approximately the same size as the doilies, and a 24" (61-mm) length of ribbon.

I cut two felt circles slightly smaller than the doilies and then hand-whipstitch one felt circle to the inside of each doily. Sometimes I weave ribbon through some of the openings in one doily and tie a bow at the top. I cut another felt circle slightly smaller than the first two circles and sandwich it between the two doilies. I tack all three pieces together at the top. I can embellish the finished case with tiny flowers, ribbons, or beads, and slip it into a birthday card.

Jeanette Johnson, Pineville, LA

HEMS

Whether you machine-stitch, serge, or hand-sew hems, you'll find lots of ways to finish them faster and more professionally in this group of hints.

Scratch-Free Netting

Netting works great to puff sleeves or to pouf out a skirt, but it can be scratchy against skin. I run the cut fabric edge through the serger, which puts a lacy soft edge on the netting.

Jo Rick,
Phelps, WI

Note from Nancy
Consider using woolly nylon thread to create an even softer edge.

A Perfect Match

When I cut out the pattern I reserve a ¼"-wide (6-mm-wide) strip about 18" to 24" long (45.7 cm to 61 cm) from the selvage of my garment fabric. When I'm ready to hem the garment, I pull a thread from the strip and am guaranteed a perfect match.
Elmerine Gantz, Palm Harbor, FL

Stitch Hems Without Knots

When turning up the hems of sleeves, skirts, etc., I zigzag or overcast each hem edge. When I get back to the beginning, I cut the bobbin thread and then pull a very long thread from the spool on top of the machine before cutting it. I thread my needle with the long thread tail and am ready to handstitch the hem without making a knot.
Kathleen McLeod, Winnipeg, Manit., Canada

Tape Soft Knits

When making leggings for my granddaughter, I like to use a double needle for the hem, but the soft knit fabric bunches up under this kind of needle. I solved this problem by sewing bias tape to each serged hem edge of the leggings before turning the hem under. Then I stitch through both the fabric and the bias tape using a double needle.
Inge Thibodeaux, Florence, MS

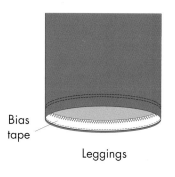

Bias tape

Leggings

Seam in Black and White

I had difficulty seeing black thread on black fabric when I was using my blindhem foot until I cut a narrow piece of Stitch-N-Tear and placed it along the hemline where the bulk of the sewing would take place. It was a breeze to stitch with black thread on top of the white strip. When the hem was finished, I pulled off the white strip. (As an alternative, place a strip of paper along the hemline.)
Anne Reid, St. Petersburg, FL

Quick Hem Easing

To ease the hem of a flared skirt, I use all four threads in my 4-thread serger to serge the bottom edge of the skirt on the right side. I then turn up the hem to the desired width and pull the *right* needle thread slightly to gather the hem. I adjust this thread until I've removed the desired amount of fullness. Then I can press and stitch the hem.
Jackie Rea, Houston, TX

Flared Skirt Hem

Note from Nancy
Run a test sample prior to serging your project. Pull the right needle thread. You may find a slightly longer stitch length will simplify easing.

Serger Surprise

The 1" (2.5-cm) hem on my daughter's flared skirt came out flat when I clean-finished the bottom with my serger. Surprisingly I didn't have to ease in any fabric. The next time I sat down at my serger I noticed that the left needle thread tension was set at +3. The next time I clean-finished the hem of a flared skirt, I purposely set my left needle thread tension on +3, and again the hem was eased in perfectly. I have done this ever since and it always comes out just right for a 1" (2.5-cm) flared hem.

Betty Kolberg, Cheraw, SC

Crisp Hems

When I'm ready to hem a garment, I fuse a strip of interfacing equal to the width of the hem on the wrong side of the garment. Since I stitch in the interfacing, no hem stitches show on the outside of the garment. This technique makes a crisp hem that hangs beautifully.

Elameda Napier, Riverton, IL

Speedy Hems

After sewing many tiny rolled hems using a hemmer foot, I've found that using a bodkin speeds the process. Before I put the hem into the sewing machine foot, I attach a bodkin to the start of the hem. I roll the fabric in ⅛" (3-mm) turns, grip the fabric with the bodkin, and apply pressure as I insert it into the hemmer foot to begin stitching.

Tammie Hagadorn, Whitehall, NY

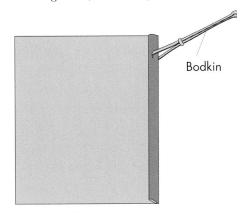

Bodkin

Rolled Hem

Softer Hems

When I use fusible thread in the lower looper of my serger, I adjust the tension so that none of the fusible thread appears on the right side of the fabric. The reason: Once fused, the thread can be scratchy against the skin.

Adjusting the tension in this way means that my serged edge is a bit unbalanced (without the upper and lower looper threads meeting exactly on the edge of the fabric), but it makes the garment more comfortable. This is especially important when I hem sleeves or the bottoms of T-shirts that I plan to tuck in.

Janet Hoxie, Seattle, WA

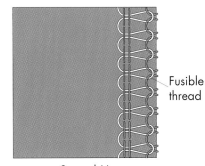

Fusible thread

Serged Hem

Keeping Pockets Free

When part of a jacket pocket falls within the jacket hem, it's easy to accidentally catch the pocket fabric when hand-sewing the hem. To avoid this, I sew the pocket to the jacket, cut an old birthday or Christmas card to the size of the pocket, and insert the card into the pocket. Then I press and hand-sew the hem. With the card insert, I don't stitch the front of the pocket to the hem.

Irene Viozzi, Burlington, Ont., Canada

Lintless Hems

When I buy a new pair of white slacks, I take out the hems and then rehem with Stitch Witchery or Wonder-Under. The webbing seals the hem so that when I launder the slacks, they don't get lint in the hemline (very noticeable in white pants).
Laura Crockett,
Beavercreek, OH

No-Show Hems

As a clothing construction teacher, I am always looking for new techniques to teach my students to make their sewing projects look more professional. As I was shortening a ready-to-wear coat this week, I stumbled onto a wonderful way to eliminate the show-through where the hem ends on heavyweight fabrics such as heavy wools and bulky corduroys. (Sometimes I get a ridge on the right side of the garment where the extra fabric thicknesses are.)

I press the hem over a hem gauge and trim the seam allowance within the hem to ¼" (6 mm). I cut a piece of hair canvas (such as Sewer's Choice from Pellon) on the bias, slightly narrower than the hem. I insert the bias-cut interfacing between the hem allowance and the garment. Then I zigzag the interfacing to the garment, ½" to ¾" (1.3 cm to 1.9 cm) from the cut edge. Finally, I hem the garment by hand, stitching through both the interfacing and the garment.

The interfacing acts as a buffer between the hem and the garment, giving body to the hem and preventing any ridge of extra fabric from showing through on the right side.
Gloria Jean Becker, South Milwaukee, WI

Weeding a Hem

A dress I made recently had a flared lower edge. The directions called for using horsehair in the bottom seam of the skirt. However, I was using a rather heavy fabric and wanted the skirt to really stand out, so I used Weed Whacker cording (from a lawn-and-garden trimmer) instead. I used my serger to stitch this cording into the seam.
Tanya Browning, Honolulu, HI

> ### Note from Nancy
> Depending on the weight of the fabric and the desired effect, you could also serge over fishing line to create this "standout" effect.

Speedy Slacks

One fold and a couple of seams make hemming slacks a breeze for me. After I've stitched the side seams, I determine the width of the slacks hem and mark this width in the seam allowances on both sides of each slacks leg. With the wrong sides out, I meet the lower hem edges of the front and the back and fold both hem edges toward the front along the hemline.

I align the side seams and restitch within the seam allowances, close to the original side seam stitching. I insert my fingers between the two hem edges and flip the top hem toward the back so that the side seams are enclosed. The hem is the correct width at the side seams, and it's a simple matter to measure, mark, and finish the remaining hem edges as desired (stitching or fusing).
Norma Ols, Lighthouse Point, FL

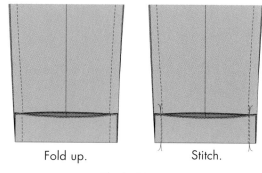

Fold up.　　Stitch.

Slacks Hem

An Alterations Secret

While working in a department store alterations division, I learned a way to trim a hem and finish the edge at the same time. When serging the hem edge to reduce bulk, instead of cutting off the hem at the desired length and then serging the edge, I simply mark the cutting position with tailor's chalk or a water- or air-soluble marker. I use shears to clip just far enough to get the serger needles in position and then serge along the mark.
Sylvia Molgren, Newton, KS

Hemming from the Top

I needed to shorten a pleated skirt, but it's virtually impossible to repress pleats at the hem. I chose to shorten the skirt at the waistline instead.

After marking the amount I needed to shorten the skirt, I placed the skirt on the ironing board, folded the pleats flat, and pinned them to the ironing board. To hold the pleats in place, I positioned a strip of Sewer's Fix-it Tape (transparent tape also works) above the shortening line and a second strip below it. Then I sewed three rows of gathering stitches over the pleats between the tape strips, stitching the rows about ¼" (6 mm) apart. I cut off the top of the skirt, eased the pleats to meet the waistband, and reattached the waistband.
Olga Lehr, David City, NE

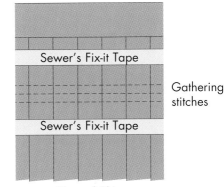

Sewer's Fix-it Tape

Gathering stitches

Sewer's Fix-it Tape

Pleated Skirt

Slip-Sliding Hems

During a recent shopping spree, I purchased some rayon fabric, forgetting how soft and slippery rayon tends to be. In the course of sewing with it, I came up with a hassle-free method of turning up and topstitching a hem. I turn up the hem 1" (2.5 cm) and press it in place. Then I cut ¾" (1.9-cm) strips of fusible stabilizer (or fusible tricot interfacing) and place a strip, fusible side up, next to the fold on the wrong side of hem. I overlock the raw edge, trimming ¼" (6 mm) of fabric.

I turn up the hem, press to fuse it in place, and topstitch the right side of the garment ⅝" (1.6 cm) from the fold. The hem will not stretch or pucker, and the fusible stabilizer adds a little weight and stability to the soft fabric.
Marguerite Wilkinson, Calgary, Alta., Canada

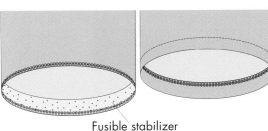

Fusible stabilizer

Hemming Rayon Fabric

A Smock from a Shirt

As a former art teacher, I know how hard it is for children to paint without getting paint on themselves as well. To make clean-up easier after my child has an art session, I made a child's painting smock from one of my husband's old long-sleeved shirts.

I cut off each sleeve just above the placket and then made a ½" (1.3 cm) casing for ¼"-wide (6 mm-wide) elastic cut slightly longer than the child's wrist measurement. Then I added rickrack to the shirt front and the cuffs. If your child has trouble buttoning the small shirt buttons, enlarge the buttonholes and replace the small buttons with larger, brightly colored ones.
Andrea Anderson, Menomonee Falls, WI

INSIDE DETAILS

Although you're not supposed to see them, properly sewn facings, linings, and shoulder pads can make your garments look tailor-made.

An Alternative Interfacing

When I need an interfacing for a sheer fabric, I use nylon netting of a compatible color. It doesn't show, gives proper stiffness, and is washable.
Betty Havlik, Sun City, AZ

Merged Facings

To eliminate bulk in facings, I tape the back facing pattern to the front facing pattern, overlapping the stitching lines and eliminating the ⅝" (1.6-cm) seam allowance. I then cut the front and back facings as one piece. This makes a smooth facing that can be interfaced the same way.
Sandra Giller, Tappan, NY

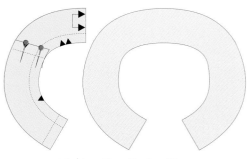

Making One Facing Piece

Note from Nancy

This technique works well on small, narrow facings. With larger facings, it might consume too much fabric. In addition, this does change the grain line, which could be a problem in some cases. If you use this technique, follow the grain line of the front facing when cutting out the modified facing.

Longer Back Facings

I think a too-narrow back facing can be one of the surest signs that a dress is home sewn. When the back facing is too narrow, this shows through the dress. I enlarge the back facing pattern, making it wider at the center back. When the dress is complete, I attach my personal label either in the middle or at the lower center back edge of the facing, where a label appears in a ready-to-wear garment.
Sharron Lamb, Renton, WA

When Woven Is Best

For blouse fronts that have the facing and the blouse front cut in one piece, nonfusible interfacing works better than fusible since it doesn't pucker or shift. First, I press the facing to the wrong side along the fold line and then unfold the facing. I position the interfacing along the fold line and stitch the outer edge with a serger or using a zigzag stitch on a conventional machine. I stitch about ¼" (6 mm) away from the fold through both the interfacing and the garment facing. (This stitching doesn't show on the finished garment, but it accurately positions the interfacing.) I start at the bottom and stitch to within 1" (2.5 cm) of the position for the top button.
Doreen Seemann, Vancouver, WA

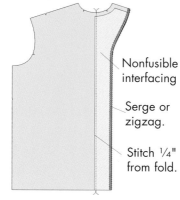

Nonfusible interfacing

Serge or zigzag.

Stitch ¼" from fold.

Blouse Front Facing

Foil Floating Fusibles

When using fusible interfacing, the bonding does not always fuse properly, leaving an interfacing that floats. Place aluminum foil under the fabric before fusing the interfacing; the reflected heat from the foil securely fuses the interfacing. The fabric receives heat from both the underside and the top. Use aluminum foil to fuse appliqués to sweatshirts as well.
Mrs. John Bleier, Nekoosa, WI, and Genevieve Travis, Takoma Park, MD

Wool's Finishing Touch

I make many wool jackets and have always thought that the little portion of the facing at the hemline looked unfinished and unprofessional, even when I overcast it with sewing thread. I examined an expensive ready-to-wear blazer and discovered that the edge had been overcast with something that seemed to disappear into the fabric. On closer inspection, I realized that the stitching must have been done with threads taken from the same fabric as the jacket. Now I pull out a few threads from the fabric and use them to overcast that little section at the bottom of the facing. With a slight steam press, the edges blend into the fabric completely.
Marnie Cameron, Chilliwack, BC, Canada

A Professional Finish for Facings

To provide a professional finish to the edges of facings, cut out the fabric and the interfacing (fusible or woven) according to pattern instructions. Stitch facing sections together at the seams then join interfacing sections at the seams.

Pin facing and interfacing, with right sides together. Trim ½" (1.3 cm) from ends and notched curved edges of interfacing to reduce bulk in the seams. Stitch a ¼" (6-mm) seam around the unnotched curved edge, clip to the stitching, and turn interfacing to the wrong side of the facing. Press with a steam iron and attach facing to the garment following pattern instructions.
Debbie Linesberry, Valrico, FL; Alice Keen, Augusta, GA; Irma Hansen, Kanwha, IA; and Ann Kinderman, Howell, MI

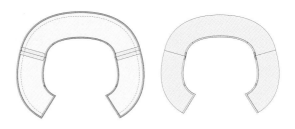

Finishing Facings

Free-Hanging Skirt Lining

I make a simple thread tack that holds a skirt lining in place without pulling on the skirt as I wear it.

After I apply the waistband and then hem both the skirt and the lining, I turn back the lining until about 3" (7.6 cm) of the skirt is exposed at the side seam. I mark this line on both the skirt and the lining, either with pins or a marking pencil, and I make a second line on the skirt seam 1" (2.5 cm) below the first mark.

I sew through one layer of the seam allowance from the second (lower) marked line to the first marked line. At the first line, I sew off the edge of the seam and chain-stitch for 1" to 1½" (2.5 cm to 3.8 cm) but do not cut the thread. I locate the marked line on the lining and stitch on the seam allowance side that faces the skirt seam, sewing up or down for about 1" (2.5 cm). Then I repeat this procedure on the other side of the skirt.
Bernice Crompton, Slayton, MN

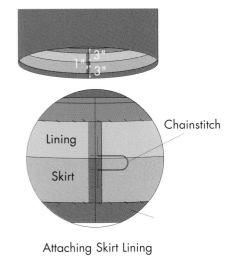

Attaching Skirt Lining

Fitting Shoulders

I have very narrow shoulders and wide hips, so I make camisoles with built-in shoulder pads to visually widen my shoulders. Then I can use size 10 patterns without altering the width of the shoulders. I make the pads from polyester fleece so that they will dry on the delicate fabric setting of my dryer as quickly as the nylon tricot camisole.
Maxine Argent, Watsonville, CA

Lines for Linings

Like many seamstresses who replace worn linings in suits and coats, I use the old lining as a pattern. To determine the grain line, I pull a thread to create a run in the old lining piece. This gives me a guide for determining the correct grain.
Kathleen Schulteis, Richfield, WI

Night Owl

I cut out and alter patterns at night when the children are asleep and I can concentrate better.
Sandy Halpin,
Lynchburg, VA

Converting to Raglan Pads

While trying to complete a dress in a hurry, I forgot to purchase or make raglan shoulder pads, so I modified ordinary ½" (1.3 cm) dress shoulder pads. Using a wide zigzag stitch, I sewed along each pad's armhole edge, compacting the pad. I ran a gathering thread along the stitched edge and gathered the pad to the desired shape. (I needed more gathering in the center.) I secured the gathering thread on each and was ready to sew my converted shoulder pads into my raglan garment.
Evelyn Armitage, Chilliwack, BC, Canada

From Shoulders to Hangers

Shoulder widths seem to change almost as much as hemlines. As a result, most of us have a collection of shoulder pads that are too good to throw away but not right for current clothes. I buy plastic hangers at a discount store and, using a few basting stitches, tack the pads to the hangers. This makes an excellent nonslip padded hanger for silks or knits. When shoulder pads are back in style, I'll simply remove them from my hangers and sew them into new garments.
Johnnene Maddison, London, Ont., Canada

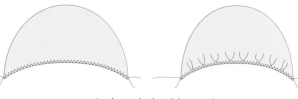

Gathered Shoulder Pads

I Do My Worst Sewing on TV! Let me explain! My machine and serger are mounted in the cabinets at a 30-degree angle so that the cameras can get a close-up of the presser foot area. I can't fully see what's going on—my best view of what's happening is to look at the monitor in front of me. In addition, I have to talk and look up at the camera while sewing. Next time you sew, try turning your machine away from you, talking, looking up while sewing, and (you'll have to imagine this part) watching a floor director's cues. I think, you'll get the idea!

Stitch Witchery Serendipity

I was making a vest lined with material that was so lightweight and slippery that no matter how I adjusted my machine tension, the stitches puckered. I didn't have any of the normal stabilizing materials available in large enough quantities, so I took a 5⁄8"-wide (1.6-cm-wide) strip of Stitch Witchery fusible bonding material and centered it over the seam line as I sewed. This provided just enough weight to solve the puckering problem.

But the real plus came when I turned the vest lining right side out and pressed the bottom and armhole edges. The Stitch Witchery fused the layers together and gave a crisp, firm edge that looked so good I didn't have to topstitch the vest at all! I tried this same technique to attach a facing to a very lightweight fabric, and in addition to eliminating the need for topstitching and understitching, the facing stayed neatly inside the garment and the seam's raw edges shouldn't ravel.
Julie Rusch, Fremont, CA

Self-Covered Pads

Especially in unlined jackets, shoulder pads can be something of an eyesore. I make shoulder pad covers from the same fabric as the garment, leaving a seam open on each cover so that a shoulder pad can be slipped inside. I attach the closed side of the shoulder pad cover to the shoulder seam before inserting a pad. I can remove pads for washing or dry cleaning, and I switch pads from one garment to another.
Marjorie Stewart, North Vancouver, BC, Canada

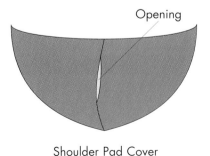

Opening

Shoulder Pad Cover

Half the Pads

When I wear a blouse with shoulder pads under a jacket or a coat with sewn-in shoulder pads, I look and feel like a football player. To overcome this problem I've made the pads in all my jackets removable. I took the pads out of the jackets, sewed the loop half of a piece of Velcro onto each jacket shoulder seam (it's softer against skin), and sewed the hook half onto a pad.
Mildred Hundley, Tempe, AZ
Other Ideas: *Norma Ols of Lighthouse Point, FL,* sews a felt strip in the shoulder seam allowances of all her clothes, using black felt on dark fabrics and white felt on light fabrics. The hook half of a piece of Velcro will attach to the felt, so she can use the same limited number of shoulder pads in all her clothes.

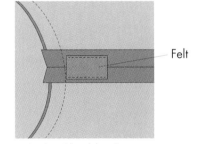

Felt

Jacket Shoulder Seam

Mary La Patka of Wilmar, MN, fuses a scrap of sweatshirt fleece (fuzzy side out) in the shoulder seams for the same purpose. *Nancy Kane of Roseville, MN,* adds nothing at all to her shoulder seams—she simply uses woolly nylon thread when serging the shoulder seams. The hook side of Velcro sticks to the woolly thread, and there's even less bulk in the seam than felt or fleece adds.

Fight the Fuzz

Just before I fuse interfacing to a fabric, I roll an adhesive lint remover lightly over the side of the fabric to be fused. This prevents raveled threads and tiny clippings from getting fused between the fabric and the interfacing, which would appear on the right side of the finished garment as small lumps and lines.
Cindy Wood, Topeka, KS

Know When to Stop

I always leave my sewing at a point where I can instantly take up where I left off. I leave an unfinished seam in the sewing machine, or if I'm handsewing, I stick the needle into the garment at the correct point and put the thimble on it. If I'm pressing, I leave the work on the ironing board or ham so that I can start just as soon as the iron warms. While I am finishing the suspended task, I refresh my mind with what needs to be done next and then proceed smoothly to the next step.
Sylvia S. Hardaway, Clearwater, FL

COLLARS, CUFFS, AND SLEEVES
If you've ever struggled to set in a sleeve or get the points on a collar just right, you'll appreciate these helpful hints!

Ribbing and Rolling

When made from soft interlock or jersey knits, my collars tend to roll forward. Now I put a single layer of ribbing knit in the band to give the collar memory. Note: The ribbing does not have to match the fabric because it's sandwiched inside the band.
Betty Fraker,
Topeka, KS

Double Crisp Collars

By looking at custom-made business shirts my husband purchased in England, I developed a technique to create professional-looking shirt collars that stay crisp even after numerous launderings.

Using a shirt pattern, I cut two pieces of fusible interfacing for the collar and then cut one of the pieces apart at the band or the fold area. I removed all the seam allowances and trimmed the area between the band and the collar to provide a ¼" (6-mm) space between the two pieces. When assembling the collar, I fused the complete interfacing piece to the collar first and then fused the two-piece interfacing on top of that.
Jacqueline Cassel-Vernon, Winnipeg, Man., Canada

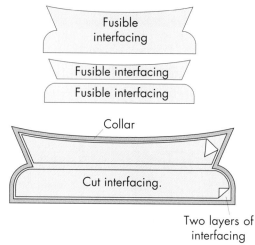

Professional-looking Collar

Stitch in-the-Ditch on Sleeves

When I sew the underarm seams of a jacket sleeve and its lining in one continuous stitching, I turn the lining to the inside and then stitch in-the-ditch at the base of the sleeve to hold the two fabrics firmly together.
Rita Jander, Hamilton, Ont., Canada

Less Is More

When making a lapel, I cut a ⅛"-wide (3-mm-wide) strip out of the interfacing along the roll line (from the dot upward). I fuse the interfacing to the jacket front, leaving the ⅛" (3-mm) area at the jacket roll line open. This makes the lapel fold easily and lie flat. The same technique works along the roll line of a collar.
Genevieve Mecherly, Madison, WI

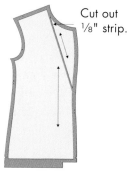

Lapel Roll Line

Quick Sleeve Placket

For an easy sleeve placket, I fuse a 1" x 2" (2.5-cm x 5.1-cm) scrap of lightweight fusible interfacing (tricot or woven) fusible side up to the right side of the sleeve placket area. Then I stitch, clip, trim, turn to the inside and press. Sometimes I topstitch around the three stitched sides. I can use this placket to finish the sleeve—it's neat and adds no bulk.
Sandy Bernstein, Madison, WI

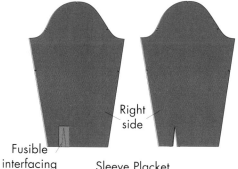

Sleeve Placket

Serger Setting Eases Ribbing

I've found a marvelous way of serging ribbing to knits. I set my serger's differential feed to the setting I use for easing fabric (since what I want to do is to speed up the front feed dogs). Then I place the longer layer next to the feed dogs, with the ribbing or the shorter layer on top. On areas such as cuffs where I have a lot of fabric in the sleeve—and particularly with a tight ribbing—this method eases the knit fabric, pulling it along faster than serging at a normal setting. I don't have to tug on the cuff and hope that my serger doesn't end up in my lap. It also uses less thread, and I avoid a rippled effect along the serged seam.
Cecilia Strong, Victoria, BC, Canada

Sharp Corners

Sometimes it's difficult to get smooth top-stitching at the corners of collars and lapels because the bulk of the fabric layers causes my machine foot to angle up. To remedy this, I use the Jean-a-ma-jig (a piece of plastic designed to help ease thick seams under a sewing machine needle) behind the foot to keep the foot level. Another option is to fold several layers of fabric and place them behind the foot to keep the foot level.
Lois Dixon, Oakville, Ont., Canada

Button-On Cuffs

I construct cuffs of a shirt, including the buttonholes, before I sew them to the sleeves. I cut out each cuff, add the interfacings, and press, wrong sides together, so that I have a defined lower edge. Then I fold under ⅝" (1.6 cm) of the seam allowance on the front and press firmly. I press ½" or 1.3 cm (slightly smaller than the front) of the back of the cuff seam allowance and topstitch ½" (1.3 cm) over the seam allowance on the front only. I turn the cuff wrong side out and stitch the side seam, angling the seam outward to the top. I turn the cuff right side out and press as though the seams were ⅝" (1.6 cm). Next I make the buttonhole. Finally, I slip the sleeve edge into the cuff and topstitch the top before completing the stitching around the entire cuff.
Eleanora Bailey, Rockwell City, IA

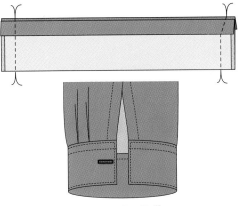

Button-On Cuff

Hands or Feet?

I cut off the knitted or ribbed tops from wornout socks. I fold the tops in half, and use them as cuffs for the ends of sleeves or legs on pajamas. Instead of hemming, I zigzag them and they don't ravel.
Marian Kiley,
DePere, WI

Soft Clothes

Don't throw away those worn clothes! Recycle the better parts of them into throw pillows. I make fancy pillows from old blouses that have lace, pintucks, or other embellishments on the front.

For the blouse pillow, I cut a blouse front to fit a pillow form, adding seam allowances and leaving the blouse closed if it buttons down the front. When I can, I use the back of the blouse for the back of the pillow; otherwise I use a coordinating fabric. I add a ruffle or gathered lace around the edges and stitch the front to the back, with wrong sides together. I turn the pillow right side out, unbutton the blouse to insert the pillow, and then rebutton. If the blouse lacks a button opening, I make an envelope-style pocket opening in the back.
Helen Hester, Jeffersontown, KY

POCKETS

Practical and sometimes decorative, this garment component can be a snap to sew once you know these viewers' secrets.

Color It Invisible

When adding pockets to the side seams of light-colored, lightweight garments, use skin-tone fabric for the top pocket section (closest to the garment front). This eliminates the color distortion of a double thickness of fabric and keeps the pocket from showing through the skirt or the pants. Use the same technique on facings for light-colored garments.
Thelma Cotellis, Bradenton, FL, and Kathryn Kessler, Collinsville, IL

Tape Instead of Pins

I am 11 years old and working on a 4-H sewing project for the fair. At one of our meetings I learned that instead of pinning a pocket on my outfit before I stitch it in place, I can just tape the pocket around the edges.
Jennifer Stoffer, Abilene, KS

Note from Nancy

Pinning a pocket in place often causes indentations that can result in uneven stitching around the pocket's edge. Using tape (like Sewer's Fix-it Tape) allows the pocket to lie flat. After topstitching the pocket, peel off the tape. Voilà! A perfect pocket.

Small Stitches Make Better Curves

I use a fabric marking pencil to trace the seam lines onto the fabric for a curved pocket. When I'm stitching the pocket, I shorten my stitch length at the curve. This helps me turn the pocket along the marked line as I sew, and the result is a great curve.
Carol S. Jones, Deltaville, VA

No More Saggy Pockets

I like to cut out the side pockets and the main garment patterns all in one piece. I've found that fusing a strip of interfacing along the pocket edge when using this technique adds stability, especially with lightweight fabrics. I get a pocket with sharp edges that won't bag or sag. The web also helps hold the pocket toward the front of the garment, keeping the pocket from facing backwards.
Marjorie Turner, Jones, OK

No More Plaid Blues

On a garment, I hate stripes and plaids that don't match or garments made of printed fabrics where the pockets don't blend into the background. My hint to prevent this is so simple that it may be in every sewing book, but it didn't occur to me until I had been sewing for more than 50 years.

I cut out the garment pieces (except the piece I want to match) and then trace the pocket or other pattern piece onto tissue or waxed paper. I place the paper over the cutout garment exactly where it is to be sewn and trace part of the print or plaid design. It's then simple to take the paper, find the correct spot on the fabric, and cut out a perfectly matched pocket or other pattern piece.
Lucy White, Indian Lakes Estates, FL

Marking Pattern to Match Plaids

A Copier to the Rescue

To get a pocket flap for a double-welt pocket precisely the desired size, I photocopy the flap pattern, place the photocopy over the fabric piece, and stitch, following the pattern's stitching line. After sewing, I remove the photocopy and finish the pocket according to the pattern guide. The stitching perforates the paper so that it comes off easily, and the pocket is the correct size to fit in the double-welt pocket opening.
Donna Fenske, Beaver Dam, WI

Prefinished Pockets

I interface a patch pocket and form rounded corners all at the same time. I clean-finish the hem edge of the pocket by zigzagging, serging, or turning under ¼" (6 mm) and topstitching. With right sides together, I turn the pocket hem to the outside of the pocket, along the fold line and press.

I cut fusible interfacing the same size as the pocket minus the hem and trim ⅛" (3 mm) from all interfacing edges. I pin the interfacing to the pocket, meeting the nonfusible side of the interfacing and the right side of the fabric. I stitch a ⅝" (1.6 cm) seam around the outer edge of the pocket before trimming the interfacing to ⅛" (3 mm) and the seam allowance to ¼" (6 mm). After I clip the corners, I turn the pocket right side out.

I carefully round out the corners, turn the hem to the inside, and fuse the edges. When I press the pocket, I have an interfaced, lined, and finished pocket, ready to be edgestitched to the garment.

Option: To make the pocket on my serger, I use a narrow 3-thread stitch, positioning the needle thread along the ⅝" (1.6 cm) seam line. As I serge, the serger trims the excess seam allowance.
Elaine Bauer, Schuler, Alta., Canada

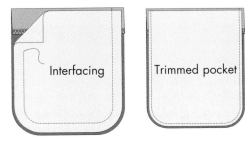

Interfaced Pocket

Note from Nancy

To get crisp edges and smooth points when I turn a pocket, I use the Bamboo Pointer & Creaser. This tool makes it much easier to obtain professional-looking corners.

Adding Pockets in Seams

When sewing pockets in the seams of a garment, I add notches where the pocket seams begin and end on both the pockets and the garment patterns. Then I stitch each pocket to the front, sewing only between the notches (not the full length of the seam with the pocket in it). I clip to the end of the stitching, turn, press, and topstitch the pocket opening.

Next I stitch the remaining pocket piece to the first pocket piece, sewing (or serging) around the outer edges. I place the garment front over the back, with right sides together, and the pocket seam away from the pinned stitching line. Stitch the side seam from the hemline to the waist, catching only the second pocket section in the seam. The seam allowance must be the same as that used to join the front pocket to the garment front. To finish, I press the seams and bar-tack at the top and the bottom of the pocket.
Lillian Moore, Morrisdale, PA

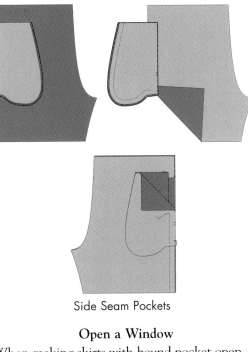

Side Seam Pockets

Open a Window

When making skirts with bound pocket openings (a pocket "window"), I clip the corners and, before turning the window, use a toothpick dipped in Fray Check to seal the clipped area and the pocket V. After the Fray Check dries, I turn the lining and have a smooth window.
Phoebe Malone, Marion, OH

Cardboard Cutouts

I make a cardboard pattern the size and the shape of a finished pocket to ensure that I get uniform pockets, reversing the cardboard to match pockets on opposite sides (right or left) of a garment. I also use the cardboard template as a pressing tool when pressing the pocket to the finished size.
Kay Ellis,
Estes Park, CO

WAISTBANDS

Viewers suggest ingenious ways to keep belts in place, hold blouses inside skirt waistbands, and sew a quicker, neater waistband.

Self-Marking Interfacing

When I interface a waistband, I place a piece of paper-backed fusible web along the fold, remove the paper backing, and place the interfacing over the web. This way, I can use the edge of the interfacing as a guide for stitching the band to the garment.
Milly Vassil, Don Mills, Ont., Canada

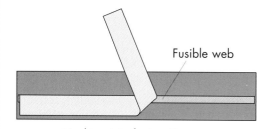

Fusible web

Marking Interfacing Placement

Hubby Help

I was making polar fleece sweatshirts for Christmas gifts but I couldn't get sturdy enough ribbing for the waistband and the cuffs. Instead I used elastic 1½" wide (3.8 cm wide) for the cuffs and 2" wide (5.1 cm wide) for the waistband inside the ribbing, secured with two rows of topstitching. I needed to stretch the elastic while topstitching but had a hard time holding the elastic to get started. After one particularly frustrating cuff, my husband suggested that I sew a tab of scrap fabric onto the edge of the elastic. This gives me a handle (similar to an anchor cloth) to pull, and when I've finished topstitching, I simply cut the tab away. (This only works if I'm working on a flat area, before I sew the side or sleeve seams.)
Janet Hoxie, Seattle, WA

Flatlock Belt Loops

Until my Mom got a serger, I wondered how the belt loops on ready-to-wear garments were made. They're flatlocked, a serger technique that works especially well on heavy fabrics like denim. I meet the lengthwise cut edges of a belt loop, with wrong sides together, and flatlock along the edges. Then I pull the tube flat and press, centering the seam. If I wish, I can edgestitch or topstitch the belt loop on the right side.
Kim Soeth, Burlington, WI

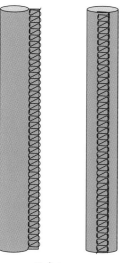

Belt Loops

Thread Belt Loops

I make fast belt loops from the thread in my sewing machine, and they always match the fabric. I pull a length of the top and bottom threads from the sewing machine, double the thread to make four strands, hold these threads taut, and zigzag over them. By threading the belt loop strands through a large-eyed needle, I can attach them to the waistline of a garment.
Eileen Jardine, Calgary, Alta., Canada

Waist Cinchers

Guess what I use to keep my blouses tucked inside my waistband? Clear elastic! For a relaxed, blousy look, I add 1" (2.5 cm) to my back waist length measurement and subtract this amount from the total back length of my blouse. From the hemline, I measure up and mark this amount all the way around on the inside of the blouse. I cut a length of clear elastic the same measurement as my waist (no need to make it tight) and apply the clear elastic to the blouse along the marked line. (I apply the elastic in the usual way: dividing the garment and the elastic into fourths, pinning the elastic in place, and stitching through the elastic.)
Marie Devine, St. John's, Nfld., Canada

Take out Basting the Easy Way

Sometimes after I apply a gathered skirt to the bodice of a dress, all or part of the lower row of gathering stitches extends below the seamline. I had trouble seeing and removing this row of stitching when I used thread that matched the garment. Now I change the color of the top thread before I sew my double row of basting (gathering) stitches, using dark thread on light fabric and light thread on dark fabric. This makes it much easier to remove the thread.
Gladys Heger, Sioux City, IA

More Give and Take

When I add a ribbed waistband or cuffs to a garment, I enclose sheer elastic in the band to give it more elasticity and to help it retain its shape.
Ethel Bullock, Oak River, Man., Canada

Ultrasuede Tabs Keep Waist Down

To keep shirts and blouses neatly tucked in, I make waistband tabs using 1½"-wide (3.8 cm-wide) strips I cut from scraps of synthetic suede such as Ultrasuede. I simply stitch the strips to the insides of waistbands at the side seams and the centers. They work as well as commercial tabs but are a lot cheaper, since many of us have suede scraps left over from other projects.
Grace Sparks, Adairsville, GA

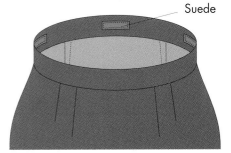

Suede

Waist Tabs

From Waist to Neck

Before discarding worn jeans, I remove the belt loops and then sew the loops to the inside neckline of jackets and sweaters to make sturdy hanging loops.
Joy Sexton, Wanatah, IN

Collage Gifts

My children often give collage kits as birthday gifts to children of nonsewers. I fill a decorative shopping bag with scraps of interesting fabrics, laces, trims, sequins, buttons, beads, and spools, along with tacky glue, scissors, and assorted paper. I've had parents tell me it was the best gift their child received.
Sandy Halpin,
Lynchburg, VA

EMBELLISHMENTS

Whether you sew for your home, for your wardrobe, or for gifts, embellishment gives you a chance to show your creativity and skill. A touch of fancy machine stitching here or a quick appliqué there, and a simple ready-to-wear garment becomes something uniquely yours.

With all the notions and sewing accessories available, embellishments that look complicated can be a snap to complete. "Sewing With Nancy" viewers have figured out novel ways to do machine embroidery, insert laces, add piping, and sew a number of other decorative elements. They have also come up with some cost-saving hints.

APPLIQUÉ

Snip a little, fuse a little, sew a little—that's all it takes to create stunning appliqués for any project.

Quick Pencil Transfer

I trace appliqué details in pencil onto the paper backing of fusible web. Then I fuse the web onto fabric and cut out the appliqué shapes, saving the paper backing. I place my appliqué faceup on a hard surface, put the paper backing with the pencil marks next to the appliqué, and rub over the design using a spoon or a fingernail. This transfers the markings to the fabric.
Lorraine Cordero, Tucson, AZ

Make Appliqué Sandwiches

When applying fusible transfer web to small, odd-shaped appliqués, place a piece of fusible web cut slightly larger than the appliqué, fusible side up, on a flat surface. Put the appliqué, right side up, on top of the web. Over both, place a piece of waxed paper (or freezer paper, shiny side down) that's larger than the appliqué; press to fuse the layers together.

After fusing, you can see through the waxed paper to cut out the appliqué. It's easy to remove the waxed paper and the web's paper backing; then apply the appliqué and embellish it.
Carol Dansak, Elizabeth, PA, and Lori Burch, Hilton, NY

Bear-ly There

I'm making an appliquéd baby quilt that has a single bear shape satin-stitched onto the center of each 6" (15.2-cm) white square. To keep from having to measure to center the bears, I cut out one bear from black fabric and fused it onto a white square to make a template. When I place a blank white square on top of this template, the black bear shows through and I can see exactly where to place the appliqué.
Mary Boggs, Florence, MS

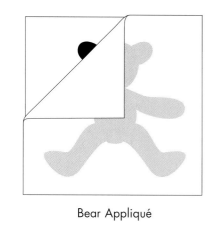
Bear Appliqué

Quick Design Transfer

I transfer a design to fabric in seconds with the unthreaded needle of my sewing machine. I place a piece of dressmaker's carbon paper (coated side down) on top of the fabric and then place the design over it. I lower the presser foot and run the unthreaded machine needle around the outline of the design.
Evelyn Donaghey, Springdale, AR

Note from Nancy

It's always wise to test this process on a scrap of fabric before using it on the real thing. Mark a design and then try removing the markings. By doing a test run, you make sure that the markings will show on the fabric and that the markings can be removed.

Temporary Stitch Lines

When I satin-stitch inner details on an appliqué, I sometimes find it next to impossible to see the actual stitching line. To outline the edge that I plan to satin-stitch, I use a disappearing-ink marker. One caution: Be sure to remove the ink with a damp cloth. Let the piece dry completely before fusing to be sure all traces of the ink have disappeared before fusing additional pieces to the design. The iron's heat could set the ink, so that it cannot be removed.
Edythe Bouck, Grand Ledge, MI

Disappearing-Ink Marker

Quick-and-Easy Appliqué

I've found an easy way to insert lace or other decorative fabric into a blouse, a handkerchief, or another project. It's a good technique for adding special touches to pockets, bibs, and children's clothing, and the appliqué design can be any shape.

First I cut a square of fusible web. I draw the design in the center of it and draw a second line ¼" (6 mm) outside the first line. For ease in cutting, I fold the square in half and cut out and discard the inside of the design.

I fuse the marked web (not the cutout center) to the wrong side of the appliqué fabric. Then I cut out the design along the traced line. This way only the narrow outer edge of the appliqué has a fusible web backing.

Next I remove the paper backing, fuse the appliqué to the base fabric, and satin-stitch around the outer edges to secure the design. I trim the base fabric under the appliqué close to the stitching, taking care not to cut the appliqué, and finish as I would any appliqué.
Carole Wardeh, Newark, DE

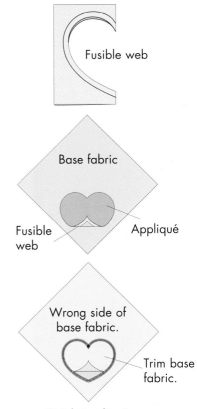

Fusible web

Base fabric

Fusible web

Appliqué

Wrong side of base fabric.

Trim base fabric.

Quick Appliqué

Use Backing to Mark

Making a Christmas top embellished with lamé, beads, and ribbon for my daughter, I pressed the lamé onto paper-backed fusible web and then traced leaves and the details (such as veins) onto the paper backing. I cut out the leaves from the lamé fabric and peeled the paper backing off the leaves.

After ironing the leaves onto the right side of the top fabric and stitching the appliqués in place, I taped the backing from the leaves onto the wrong side of the fabric, placing each leaf backing on the outline of the appliquéd leaf. Using a very small zigzag stitch and sewing from the wrong side of the fabric, I stitched along the vein lines, tore away the paper, and turned the fabric to the right side. The leaf details were easy to see on the lamé, so I could satin-stitch over my small zigzag stitches, using metallic silver thread to appliqué the leaves and teal metallic to highlight the details.
Marie Scott, Prospect Park, PA

Note from Nancy

Use a size 80 metafil needle when using metallic thread. The needle has a large elongated eye to avoid thread stripping and a specialized scarf that helps eliminate skipped stitches.

See the Appliqué

I find it easy to obtain correct placement of appliqué pattern pieces when the pattern is transparent. I copy my patterns only onto transparency film. On the copier I use, I feed the transparency film (which is heaver than copy paper) into the machine manually rather than using a tray.
Cindy Bode, Placentia, CA

Stained Glass Patterns

Books with designs for stained glass light-catchers contain excellent appliqué patterns. I used one floral design on a T-shirt. Using a photocopy machine, all I had to do was enlarge or reduce the design to whatever size I preferred.
Christine Jack,
Victoria, BC, Canada

More Hold, Less Web

Fusible web is great for securing an appliqué to a project before satin-stitching around the outer edges, but sometimes web makes a large appliqué too stiff. As an option, I temporarily secure an appliqué to a garment using ThreadFuse. I position a strand of ThreadFuse between the appliqué and the base fabric, very close to the outer edge of the appliqué. Then I cover the fabric layers with a press cloth and use a steam iron to fuse small sections (several inches at a time) until the entire appliqué is attached. The ThreadFuse secures the appliqué to the base fabric so that the fabric layers don't shift as the appliqué is stitched in place.
Mary Reynolds, Surprise, AZ

Make a Blooming Blouse

For a personalized blouse, I take apart silk flowers, remove the wire from each petal, iron them flat, and arrange them on the blouse. I then apply the flowers to the garment using fusible web. To complete each flower, I outline the petals with paint and add a bead or a rhinestone in the center using fabric glue.
Julia Morgan, Hudson, FL, and
Victoria Derybowski, Whiting, IN
Another Idea: To ornament a fine white top or dress, *Ellie Senne of Allison, IA,* buys a stem of organdy leaves from the bridal section of her favorite fabric store. Instead of fusing the petals to the garment, she carefully positions them and then satin-stitches around the edges. She cuts off the back layer of fabric (the original garment), leaving a sheer, white-on-white flower.

Note from Nancy

To prevent the fusible web from sticking to the ironing board or the underside of your iron when attaching the petals, use an appliqué pressing sheet. After cutting a piece of fusible web the size of a petal and positioning the web against the back side of the petal, sandwich the petal inside a folded appliqué pressing sheet. After the petal has cooled, remove it from the pressing sheet. Then cut around the petal, remove the excess web, and fuse the petal to the garment.

Make Flags Fly

I was making a quilt and wanted to give appliquéd checkered flags the appearance of being blown in the breeze. Here's what I did: I cut a square of checkered fabric, dampened the fabric, and stretched it on the bias while pressing it with a hot iron. I immediately applied fusible web to the back of the fabric, fused it in place, and then satin-stitched the appliqué to the base fabric.
Tindy MacBain, Ann Arbor, MI

Flag Appliqué

Appliqué Templates

Whenever I want a certain portion of a fabric to be in a particular position in a completed appliqué, I first cut a template of the design from clear plastic. Placing that template over the fabric before I trace, I can see exactly where the desired portion will be in the finished appliqué.
Lydia Estoye, Polk City, FL
Another idea: *Ina Fay Goracke of Camp Verde, AZ,* paints clear nail polish around the outer edges of her templates. This gives each template a sharp, visible edge and helps keep it from being nicked out of shape.

No More Slippery Appliqués

To make appliqués from a fabric that ravels a lot (such as satin), I stabilize the fabric before cutting by using a liquid wash-away stabilizer. I apply a thin layer of stabilizer to the fabric and let it dry. (You can speed the drying by using a hair dryer.) Then I cut out and fuse the appliqué as usual. I can easily remove the stabilizer after stitching by laundering or by immersing the project in water.
Angela Wewel, Lakewood, CO

A Tacky Solution

I do a lot of appliquéing in my cottage industry and had some problems with my hands slipping on the fabric at the wrong time while sewing. Having been in banking for years gave me the solution: From an office supply store I buy Tacky-Finger, a glycerine product usually used to speed turning pages or counting paper money, and use it to moisten my fingers before I start a project and while sewing. It works like a charm for appliquéing and for sewing slippery fabric!

LaWanna Childs, Lumbertson, TX

Gripping Stencils

To make stenciling easier, cut the stencil out of Grid Grip or freezer paper rather than plastic. Simply press the nongrip or shiny side of the stencil onto the fabric and apply paint. Just remember to peel off the stencil before the paint dries!

Delight Snyder, Apollo, PA, and
Mary Jane Yancey, Sumter, SC

Wear Your Heart on Your Sleeve

Here's a tip that isn't the least bit practical, but it does get to the heart of things! On every top that I make for myself, I hand- or machine-embroider a tiny heart somewhere on a sleeve—sometimes visible and sometimes hidden inside the cuff. This is my special reminder to myself that we all need peace in our hearts.

Sandy Tillotson,
Mareton, NJ

What's my favorite item to sew?

When I think about what I've sewn over the past year, I'm amazed at the number of jackets I've made. No, not the lined version, but classic styles that are easy to sew and could, if I wanted, lend themselves to a touch of creativity. On TV you see my jackets or tops, not my pants or skirts. (I have a basic black skirt that I've worn on TV too many times to mention!) I wear jackets to work, on TV, when I give seminars, and even over a pair of jeans. Basically, a jacket is my favorite wardrobe piece.

My other main sewing projects are gifts. Instinctively, when a friend or family member is getting married or has a new baby, I think, "Oh, I'll make them a quilt!" It's a little joke I have with myself, because there aren't enough hours in a day for me to create all those quilts. Now shower and wedding gifts are along the line of serged napkins and table runners; baby gifts are simple rompers with a fun appliqué something that can be sewn in an evening.

DECORATIVE STITCHING

Use your machine to embellish a purchased blouse, add metallic accents to garments, and dress up virtually any sewing project.

Fringed Designs

For charted needle decorations, I allow a ¼" to ½" (6-mm to 1.3-cm) border around the edges of my appliqué and then fringe the fabric edges. Fringes can be short or long (depending on the margin you left unstitched), adding variety to the decorations.
Agnes Hofer,
Lewiston, ID

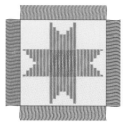

Fringed Edges

Faux Blanket Stitches

When attaching appliqués, I give the appearance of blanket stitching by using a blindhem stitch. After I fuse the appliqué to the fabric, I place cotton batting on the wrong side. I adjust the machine for a blindhem stitch using a short stitch length; then I put thread that contrasts with my fabric into both the needle and the bobbin. This saves considerable time over blanket-stitching by hand.
Karen Guffey, Newton, IA

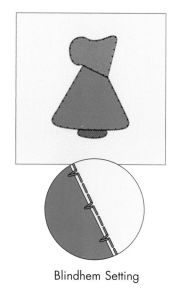

Blindhem Setting

Serged Monograms

I use my serger to make fast and easy monograms. I put fusible thread in the lower looper and decorative thread in the upper looper. Then I serge over ⅝" (1.6-cm) Seams Great to make decorative thread tails. I arrange the thread tails into monograms on towels, fashion garments—wherever I wish. Then I fuse them to the project and use a conventional sewing machine threaded with clear monofilament thread to zigzag the monograms in place.
Donna Fenske, Beaver Dam, WI

From Copier to Iron to Garment

Photocopies make great iron-on transfers. They can be ironed to the right side (which reverses the image) or to the wrong side of fabric and will generally wash out. Test a sample if you are unsure.

If you want to reverse a design before making an iron-on transfer, trace the design onto tracing paper with a black marker and then turn the paper over and retrace the design onto the back. You can photocopy the wrong side of the tracing paper to make an iron-on transfer.

Another easy way to get a reverse image is to iron the photocopy onto organdy. You can turn the organdy over and see the reversed design through the organdy. Then apply the organdy by machine embroidery to the project.
Linda Adkins, Franklin, MA

You Ought to Be in Pictures

I use my computerized sewing machine's single patterns and pattern elongation keys along with different thread colors to put together small embellishments that look especially attractive on pockets. By combining oval, round, and crescent stitches, I can sew accents such as birds and ladybugs and mushrooms nested in leaf-shaped stitches.
Gail Stafford, Lockport, NY

Kitchen Help

I trace the designs from kitchen paper towels onto tear-away stabilizer and use them as patterns for machine embroidery. The large designs are perfect for decorating pillows and pillowcases, and smaller parts of the design work well on collars, cuffs, and pockets. I've used the side border designs on ribbons for hair bows, on bed linens, and down the front of a blouse placket that hides buttons.
Sandy Botfield, Sonora, CA

Straight Blanket Stitches

To get hand-done blanket stitching that looks as even as the machine blanket stitching I see on ready-to-wear garments, I start by top-stitching in a contrasting color with a basting stitch (approximately seven stitches per inch) about ½" (1.3 cm) from the outer edge. Using the topstitching as a guide, I use embroidery floss to make a blanket stitch every third basting stitch. This eliminates having to measure every stitch, and I simply remove the top-stitching when I've finished sewing.
Ann Oravec, Harper Woods, MI

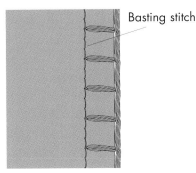

Basting stitch

Blanket Stitch Trim

Another idea: *Linda Talley of Waco, TX,* tears the perforated edges from computer paper and pins a strip to the edge of a project she plans to blanket stitch. The holes in the paper serve as her stitch guides, and when she's done, she cuts the outside edge of each hole and lifts off the paper.

Quick Cards

I add machine decorative stitches to note-papers, greeting cards, envelopes, and recipe cards, using fine threads and needles so that the paper isn't weakened. Sometimes I knot and clip the loose thread ends, and sometimes I secure them with a glue stick or a tiny dot of white glue.
Charlene Ray, Waterville, ME

No-Sew Embroidery Trim

For a different finish for a collar or a cuff, top-stitch along the edge and then weave six strands of embroidery floss in and out of the stitches to make a wavy effect. Embroidery floss is packaged with six strands wound together, so simply thread all six strands through a needle and weave.
Shirley VerHage, Waupun, WI

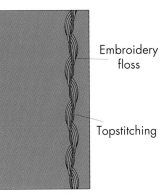

Embroidery floss

Topstitching

Woven Trim

Texturize Satin Stitches

When satin-stitching using variegated thread, I find that adding crochet thread as a cord under the satin stitching gives the finished product more texture and dimension.
Fran Walton,
Vernon Hill, VA

Fill in the Blanks

Many preprogrammed embroidery patterns are in outline form. I achieve a different effect by painting the enclosed areas in colors of my choice, using fabric markers or paints.
Rosemary Szul, Sarasota, FL

Something from Nothing

My sewing machine can only do straight stitching and zigzag stitching; it doesn't have a decorative stitch capability, so I decided to improvise. I used a double needle with two different colors of thread and set my machine for its widest and longest zigzag stitch. Then I sewed on the wrong side of a lining. When I turned the lining over, what showed on the right side was a lovely decorative stitch.
Marilyn Brown, Lutz, FL

Note from Nancy

Before you try this technique, check the swing of the double needle to make certain one or both of the points will not hit the sewing machine throat plate as the needle zigzags back and forth. Turn the wheel by hand for a few stitches to make certain the width of the throat plate hole is sufficient for the double needle zigzag. If it's not, the needle could break.

Check the Back

After I tried different decorative stitches on my sewing machine, I turned my fabric over and discovered that I had a lovely and delicate embroidery stitch on the wrong side. I decided to use the stitch on the collarless blouse I was making. On the wrong side of the fabric, using a double needle, I stitched all around the neckline and down the front so that the embroidery appears on the right side.
Marguerite Brien, Largo, FL

Hoop Dreams

I make a hoop for machine embroidery by cutting out the plastic cover and rim of any round container (margarine tubs, whipped topping tubs, potato chip cans, etc.). When I'm through using them for hoops, I can insert a piece of embroidered fabric into the hoop, glue lace around the edge, and have an attractive Christmas ornament.
Jean Lanzillo, Tempe, AZ

Identical Pintucks

A fast and easy way to make identical-width pintucks is to use a blindhem foot. I move the needle position so that the distance between the needle and the blindhem foot guide is the desired pintuck width, and then I set my machine for straight stitching. When I place the fold of the fabric next to the guide of the blindhem foot, the foot helps guide the fabric and maintains an even pintuck width as I sew. Sometimes I have to adjust the thread tension, depending on the fabric weight.
Heidi Doyle, Phoenix, AZ

Pintuck Foot to the Rescue

When doing charted needlework, I keep my rows of stitching parallel and prevent broken needles by guiding the charted needlework needles through an appropriately sized pintuck foot.
Ann Gervasio, Herndon, VA

Something Extra

Whenever I stitch a pintucked strip to be used in a dress, I make it bigger than necessary. When I trim the excess pintuck strip after it's inserted into the garment, I have leftover scraps large enough to use elsewhere. Sometimes I shape them into hearts, ovals, and diamonds, and appliqué them onto garments. I use very tiny scraps when making doll clothes.
June Eveker, St. Louis, MO

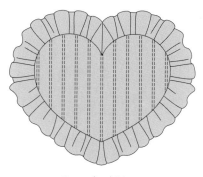

Pintucked Heart

Color It Washable

I've found that Crayola Washable Markers are wonderful markers to use for transferring designs for machine embroidery. When I finish the embroidery, I wash the fabric in cold water, and the markings come out instantly. The only color of fabric that these markers do not work on is black. The Crayola container says normal laundering should remove marker stains from cotton, polyester, acrylic, and nylon fabrics and their blends.
Blanche Rehling, Millstadt, IL

Note from Nancy

Test a fabric sample with the marker to be certain it does wash out. Not all fabrics respond the same way to washable markers.

A New Use for Tulle

I use a permanent marking pen to copy an embroidery or fabric painting design onto a piece of tulle. Then I place the tulle on the fabric where I want to add the design and trace over the pattern with a fabric marker. The fine mesh of the tulle lets the markings go through to the fabric. When I remove the tulle, the pattern shows clearly on the fabric. This technique is quick and easy, and I can reuse the pattern many times.
Betty Davis, Kimberling City, MO

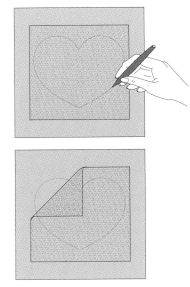

Tulle Pattern

Hidden Thread Tails

To secure the threads when satin-stitching or for any close zigzag stitching, I pull the bobbin thread up through the fabric before beginning to sew. I hold the top and bobbin threads together and zigzag over them a short distance. Then I clip both thread ends and continue to stitch. There are no threads on the bottom to tie or to clip, making a neat finish.
Charlene Gray, Metamora, IN

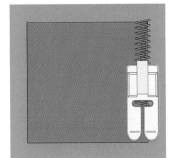

Securing Threads

Picking Up Where You Left Off

When I'm sewing in the middle of a programmed design on my computerized sewing machine and the thread breaks or the power is interrupted, it's hard to resume stitching at that exact spot. I've used a scrap of fabric to stitch until I reached that point and then switched to the project, but sometimes the fabric scrap slips.

Then I remembered the old days (before computers) when I typed on a typewriter. If I had to remove paper to make a correction, I set the ribbon indicator to "stencil" and could strike several times without putting ink on the paper. I do the same thing now with my sewing machine. I remove the thread from the needle only, leaving the bobbin and the rest of the machine threaded. Then I sew slowly, watching closely until the needle reaches the spot where I stopped. I rethread the needle and continue without any jumps in my stitching pattern.
Frances Charles, Vicksburg, MS

Hold Those Stitches

To keep rayon thread used in machine embroidery from raveling when a garment is laundered, I fuse interfacing (with the edges pinked) to the back of the embroidery. The interfacing not only eliminates raveling, it also covers the unsightly thread ends.
Karen Sims,
Nine Mile Falls, WA

Machine Seed Stitches

I make a seed stitch on my machine by adjusting the tension so that the bobbin thread comes to the top of the fabric, creating tiny dots. I experimented by embroidering the same design three times, using the same variegated thread in the needle each time, but with three different colors of bobbin thread—light green, bright yellow, and off-white. There was quite a difference!
Sunny Greenwood, Orange, CA

Quick Change

I have a young son and daughter and I enjoy sewing for both of them. Sometimes, however, I lack the time to make a complete outfit. Last year, I took one of my daughter's white blouses with a Peter Pan collar and scallop-stitched around the outside edge using a contrasting color thread. This was very simple and only took a short time, but it gave a beautiful feminine touch to her blouse for Easter. And I felt good to have added Mom's touch!
Jackie Johnson, Lenexa, KS

Timing Is Everything

Adding decorative stitching after a garment is constructed can be difficult. Also, the stitching may draw up the fabric, making the garment smaller than it was originally. It's much easier to machine-stitch on flat fabric before cutting out the garment. I choose the pattern pieces that I want to embellish and mark the correct placement of the decorative stitching on the fabric. When all my decorative stitching is complete, I cut out the pattern and construct the garment as usual.
Sue Rumpf, New Berlin, WI

Colorful Entredeux

Sometimes when I want extra color in entredeux, I weave embroidery floss through the openings.
Jane Strader, Springfield, IL

Mirror, Mirror . . . .

After completing a nightgown with rather large tucks, I decided to accent it with a decorative stitch. I selected the stitch and added it to the tucks on one side of my nightgown. Then I realized I couldn't mirror the stitch, since my machine doesn't have mirroring capability. I left it for the night and woke up with the solution.

The bobbin provides the mirror image of my sewing machine stitch. I filled the bobbin with embroidery thread, loosened the tension on the bobbin, tightened the upper tension, and sewed on the wrong (back) side of my tucks. Voilà! The image was mirrored. (Remember, this won't work with double needles, and be sure to reset your tension before continuing sewing.)
LaRae Johnson, Mt. Lehman, BC, Canada

Playtime Inspires Children

I always keep several 3" x 15" (7.6-cm x 38.1-cm) strips of scrap fabric near my sewing machine so that they're readily available whenever any of my four children or their friends wish to try out my sewing machine. And I do encourage them to sew with all the fancy stitches! It's fun for all of us, and the children treat the machine with respect. This is often the only chance most of their friends get to run a sewing machine.
Paula White, Viola, WI

Note from Nancy

Letting children try out a sewing machine is a great way to get them involved in sewing at an early age. However, for their safety and for the safety of your machine, it's a good idea to keep a close watch on youngsters while they use the machine.

Check It Off

To help me avoid rushing at the last minute to meet a project deadline, I keep a schedule of projects pinned to the wall above my sewing machine, dividing projects into short-term and long-term. Each project is listed with a due date and a rating ("B" for big projects and "L" for little ones).

I check projects off as I complete them and add new listings as necessary. This discourages me from starting new projects until the big ones are finished. (It also discourages me from buying more fabric!)

Carrie Ferguson, Enfield, NS, Canada

Pipe Down (and Up)

When you're making a coordinated blouse, skirt, and jacket, add piping to accent the lapel, the seams, and the pockets of each. Make your own piping, using various colors from the printed or patterned fabric of the coordinating garments. It's an easy way to create a real designer look!

Mavis Wyre, Jacksonville, FL

Customizing Blouses

While planning what to wear on a trip, I found that I needed a blouse to coordinate with a dinner jacket that was accented with gold trim, so I embellished the bib section of a blouse from my wardrobe. I marked stitching lines with a washable pen and stitched along the lines with a decorative machine stitch. I placed Wash-Away stabilizer under the fabric and then hand-stitched beads onto part of the design to give it sparkle. As I stitched the beads, I wove the thread under the bobbin thread between the stitched areas. It added a designer touch in very little time.

Ginny Jovanovich, Sussex, WI

No More Whiskers

I like to use my sewing machine's scallop stitch. On one of your shows, you recommended sewing off the fabric onto adding machine tape as a stabilizer, but I was disappointed because the paper showed through the darker colors of thread I used. I decided to try thin construction paper. It worked beautifully because I could match the color of paper to the color of thread I used. I found it also tears away much easier than adding machine tape.

Norma Reed, Hardin, NY

Serge a Strap

I used a serger technique to make a strap for an evening bag. I put cranberry rayon thread in the loopers and all-purpose serger thread in the needle and serged over iridescent ribbon floss. The strap matches my cranberry Ultrasuede bag perfectly and is strong enough to support an evening bag.
Beverly Toret,
Jeannette, PA

EDGINGS

Topstitching, piping, bias binding—you'll find lots of help for all sorts of decorative edgings in these hints from "Sewing With Nancy" viewers.

"Handstitched" by Machine

For topstitching with a handstitched look, use the straight stretch stitch on your machine. No need to use a heavier-than-normal thread.
Ramona Ruggeri, Norris, IL

A Big Match for Little Money

There are times when I need to repair small areas of topstitching. Even though the job doesn't require much thread, I do need a near-perfect color match, and I find it wasteful to purchase a whole spool of thread that I'll probably never use again. Instead I buy a skein of embroidery floss, available in so many colors that I'm sure to find a match. I remove one strand equal to the length I think I'll need (just clip and pull it right out) and wind it around any empty spool and bobbin. It works beautifully and the cost is minimal.
Gertrude Viveiros, Sunnyvale, CA

Another idea: *Marie LaCroix of Lively, Ont., Canada*, uses six strands of embroidery floss in the bobbin for topstitching. She finds it works best to wind the bobbin by hand to prevent the floss from twisting or tangling. She then loosens the bobbin tension slightly and sets the machine at seven or eight stitches per inch. She topstitches with the right side of the garment facedown and always stitches a sample before working on the garment.

Topstitching Serged Seams

I wanted to accent the yoke of a fleece jacket with decorative topstitching, but my flatlock stitch does not lie flat. Instead of flatlocking, I serged a regular seam in a contrasting color thread with wrong sides together and then used my conventional machine to topstitch the serged seam allowances flat against the garment. With monofilament nylon thread in the needle, I used the narrow rolled hem foot to hold the serged ridge vertical and then to flatten it out under the needle so that I could catch the very edge of the seam.
Annette Hornbacher, Jerome, ID

Double Your Thread

For decorative topstitching, I replace the single spool of thread on top of my machine with two bobbins, each containing a different color of thread. Then I thread as usual, bringing both threads through the machine, and thread the bobbin with thread matched to the fabric.
Sharon Bujak, Buffalo, NY

Make Bindings with Memory

When binding sleeveless and collarless tops or jumpers, I use ribbing or good-quality double knit instead of bias tape. It is so easy and quick, and it also gives memory to the edges.

I cut ribbing 1½" (3.8 cm) wide and place the right sides of the garment and the ribbing together. I overcast the edges, stretching the ribbing to match the fabric. I stitch a ½" (1.3-cm) seam with a straight stitch or a narrow zigzag. Then I fold the binding over the edge to the inside of the garment and topstitch from the right side. I sometimes use a double needle or a fancy stretch stitch, catching both the binding edge and the garment. I then trim the excess binding on the inside.

I use this technique on stretch and woven fabrics. It's a great way to coordinate jumpers with T-shirts, using T-shirt fabric around the jumper's neckline and armholes. I also use it around skirt hems.
Rosemary Fiedrich, Kamloops, BC, Canada

Pseudobraid on Boiled Wool

As an alternative to braid, I finish the outer edges of boiled wool garments on my serger using a heavy thread (such as pearl cotton or Metropearl) or a type of narrow ribbon (such as ribbon floss) in both the upper and lower loopers. I set the stitch at the widest setting and use a medium stitch length. This technique results in a very attractive finish.
Susan Schleif, Clearwater, FL

Easy Binding

A machine quilter in Lincoln taught me this clever way to bind bedspreads. It is useful for binding any edge, including those on pillows, place mats, and such.

I cut a 2¾"-wide (6.7-cm-wide) bias strip of fabric and fold the strip in half. On the right side of the project, with the cut edges meeting, I stitch the strip to the project with a ¼" (6-mm) seam allowance. Finally I fold the bias strip over the cut edge and handstitch the folded edge over the seam line.
Mary Carlson, Waverly, NE

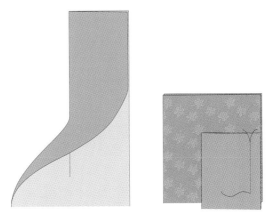

Binding

Stitching Stability

I made a shell blouse out of tissue faille, and when I topstitched the sleeve and bottom hems with a double needle, the stitching was uneven. The fabric slid around even though I had pinned each edge; no matter how I adjusted my tensions, the stitching remained uneven.

Finally I cut strips of used clothes dryer sheets and put them on the back of the fabric, with the dryer sheet next to the feed dogs. This stabilized the fabric, keeping the tension even and preventing the fabric from slipping around as I stitched. After stitching, I trimmed the sheet from the back of the hem. This not only gave the stitching stability but also made the hem look crisp.
Ann Chan, Tucson, AZ

Trim Sewing Time

By using this easy technique I cut my time in half when sewing bias trim and a ruffle or lace to a baby blanket or a place mat. With wrong sides together, I meet the cut edges of the ruffle and the project. Then I pin bias tape to the same edge, wrong side up. Beginning ⅝" (1.6 cm) from the cut edge, I sew along the crease of the bias trim. When I reach the starting point, I fold under the cut edge of the bias tape and overlap the free end. Next I join both ends of the ruffle to conceal the raw edges and then finish stitching.

I finger-press the trims to the right side, pin them in place, and secure the bias trim by hand or by machine, or I use a decorative machine stitch to spice up the trim. Try this technique to give your place mats and baby blankets a different look from either side.
Jerrie Fry, Yuba City, CA

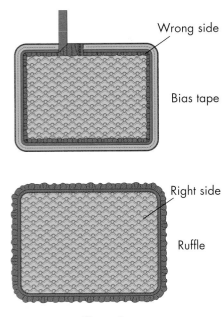

Bias Ruffle and Trim

Get Out a Notebook

Narrow-lined paper is marked exactly ¼" (6 mm) apart, so I pin it to fabric and use it as a guide for topstitching at that interval.
Lucile M. Olson, Traverse City, MI

Fused Bias Edgings

Use fusible thread to fuse-baste the underside when applying bias binding. To make ½"-wide (1.3-cm-wide) finished tape, cut 3"-wide (7.6-cm-wide) bias strips. Instead of folding the raw edges to the center, fold the tape in half and press so that the cut edges meet. Set up a conventional sewing machine with fusible thread in the bobbin. With right sides together and cut edges meeting, stitch the folded bias strip to the garment with a ½" (1.3-cm) seam. Then finger-press the bias binding up and over the cut edge so that it covers the fusible thread on the back side. When pressed, the tape is securely positioned. Then you can stitch in-the-ditch through the seam well from the right side to permanently attach the binding or top-stitch the binding in place.
Janet Klaer, Stamford, CT, and Lily Fong, San Jose, CA

Glue Braid in Place

While attempting to sew a decorative braid in a swirl and loop design on a suit jacket, the braid kept shifting under the sewing machine foot on the curves. Finally I used dabs of glue stick and some pins to anchor the braid where I wanted it. Then I set my machine up for free-motion quilting. Great! The braid didn't shift, and I didn't have to continuously turn my jacket to feed the braid under the presser foot. Even though my stitches weren't even, no one could tell because my thread matched the braid.
Victoria Konrady, West Des Moines, IA

Lengthen Stitch for Serger Braids

Once when I was chaining on my serger to make matching braid for a project I forgot to shorten the stitch length. I had set up my serger for a rolled edge, put pearl cotton in the upper looper, crochet cotton in the lower looper, and all-purpose serger thread in the needle. I serged several yards of this braid using a stitch length of 3.8. I found that with the longer stitch length, the serger chain looks more like it was actually braided.
Beverly Toret, Jeannette, PA

Contrast Ribbing Accents Knits

I purchased some knit fabric for a top and was unable to find ribbing to match. I used contrasting color ribbing for the neckline, trimmed with fabric from the shirt. This technique also works great for pockets and sleeves.

I cut a strip of contrasting color ribbing and then cut the strip in half lengthwise. I cut a 1"-wide (2.5-cm-wide) strip of garment fabric with the greatest stretch along the length of the strip. Then I serged the self-fabric between the two ribbing strips, using a ¼" (6-mm) seam allowance. I joined the ends of the band and folded the band in half lengthwise. Then I quartered both the band and the garment and attached the band to the garment as for traditional ribbing.
Darlene Delany, Salem, OR

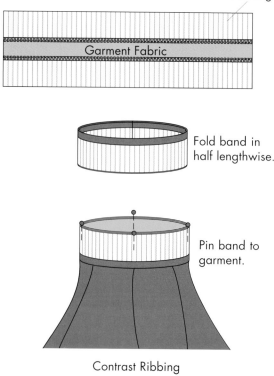

Ribbing

Garment Fabric

Fold band in half lengthwise.

Pin band to garment.

Contrast Ribbing

Note from Nancy

Before stitching the knit fabric to the ribbing, pin the ends of the fabric together, forming a circle. Slip the circle over your head to test for stretchability.

Quick Ultrasuede Fringe

To cut Ultrasuede fringe using a rotary cutter and a mat, I start with a length of Ultrasuede fabric as wide as I want the finished fringe to be plus ½" (1.3 cm). Then I tape approximately ½" (1.3 cm) of the fabric to the back of the cutting mat and wrap the remaining fabric to the front (cutting side) of the mat. I secure the Ultrasuede edges with double-sided tape (carefully choosing a tape that won't leave a sticky residue on the surface). I protect the surface under the mat from accidental cuts, place a quilting ruler on the Ultrasuede, and then cut up and off the Ultrasuede. When the fringe is complete, I remove the tape and have perfectly straight and evenly cut fringe.

With this method, I can accurately cut fringe as narrow as ⅛" (3 mm). I either insert a ½" (1.3-cm) Ultrasuede header into a seam or stitch it on top of the garment using decorative threads (even metallics). The decorative stitches look like expensive coordinated trim.
Kathy Smith, Colleyville, TX

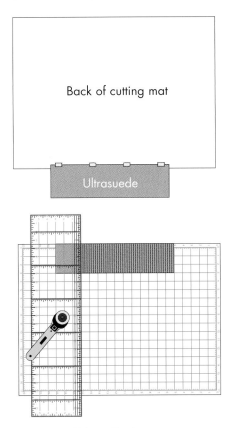

Fringe Cutting

Quick Lacy Edging

I've been sewing preemie baby clothes, and I use the 3-thread overlock on my serger to finish the edges fast. But for baby girls' garments, I prefer a lacy edge. I could stitch lace on by hand or by machine, but this takes a lot of time. Also the color and pattern selection of narrow laces is limited. Instead I serge the edge and then zigzag over the serged edge. This gives a lacy look to the edge and is great for me, since my sewing machine doesn't do fancy stitches like the new computerized machines.
Larry Costello, Two Harbors, MN

Invisible Binding Seams

To disguise the point where bias binding ends meet, stitch the cut edge of bias binding to the right side of the item in the usual manner, leaving 2" to 5" (5-cm to 12.7-cm) tails of binding free at both ends. Stop stitching several inches from the point where the binding ends will meet (leaving a short section unstitched) and fold the free edges where the ends meet to form a miter. Crease the fabrics, mark the crease with a pencil, and stitch the two ends together, following the marked line. Stitch the remaining section of the binding to the item. The place where the binding started and ended looks like any other binding seam.
Marilyn Fils, Creston, IA, and
Daphne Stewart, Sunnyside, WA

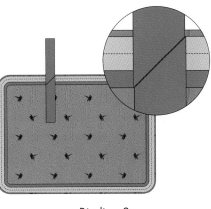

Binding Seam

Stronger Piping Cord

When I make piping for yokes, collars, or cuffs, I first pull the cord through beeswax. The wax stiffens the cord, making it easier to handle and to control.
Jackie Beck,
Glenwood, AR

A Secret Revealed

For many years I've been using a special trick for adding color-coordinated trim to cuffs and collars on dresses and blouses in lieu of topstitching. No one's ever figured out how I do it. Here's the trick: I chainstitch with a crochet hook and a skein of embroidery floss, using all six strands. I press the chain, being careful to keep it even so that I can see the attractive chain side. Then I simply top-stitch the chain to the edges of collars or cuffs, or create a design on the garment with the chain.
Josephine Walmsley,
Scottsdale, AZ

Bias Tape from Scraps

To make variegated bias tape out of scraps, I cut long strips from three or four different fabrics. The width of each strip can be the same as all the others or it can vary between 1" and 4" (2.5 cm and 10.2 cm). I sew or serge the strips together with ¼" (6-mm) seams and press all the seams in one direction. I fold one corner of the joined strips in half by meeting a vertical edge to a horizontal edge, forming a right angle, and then cut along the fold. (The cut line is a true bias.) From this variegated fabric, I can then cut bias strips to the desired size, using a cutting mat and a rotary cutter and measuring from the cut edge.
Mumtaz M. Dewji, White Rock, BC, Canada

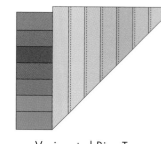

Variegated Bias Tape

Timely True Bias

When cutting continuous bias strips (the kind made by cutting in a spiral around a tube of fabric) from a silky fabric, I've found that this type of fabric tends to change shape dramatically once I lift the strips from the cutting surface. To save time and increase accuracy, I not only cut the original parallelogram using a rotary cutter, but I also use the rotary cutter to actually cut the lines to within 2" (5.1 cm) of the seam line. I pin the bias edges together, offsetting the fabric ends by the width of one strip. Then I stitch and press. To finish, I simply cut across the 3½" (8.9 cm) of fabric adjacent to the seam—a very easy task with 5" (12.7 cm) or longer shears. Voilà! A bias strip of consistent width, without the need to mark or hand-cut yards of fabric!
Nancy Restuccia, Minneapolis, MN

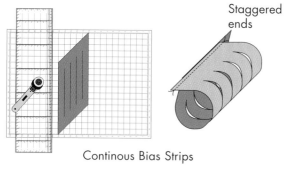

Staggered ends

Continous Bias Strips

Ruffled Ribbing Cuffs

I came up with this idea quite by accident. I had a nightgown with stretched-out elastic at the wrists and decided to replace the elastic with ribbing that wouldn't ride up as much as the elastic when I was reading in bed. The result is a sleeve treatment that I'll use on new tops—it finishes each sleeve with ribbing and a ruffle all in one seam.

I made a narrow hem at the bottom of each sleeve. Then I determined the ruffle width I wanted, folded back the lower edge of the sleeve to the ruffle width (with right sides together), and pressed. I cut ribbing double the desired width (wider than the ruffle if I want it to extend beyond the ruffle), and stitched it into a cylinder. Then I folded it and quartered it. I quartered the sleeve at the fold line, matched quarter marks with the ribbing, and stitched the ribbing to the sleeve, stretching it as I stitched. When I folded the ruffle down, the cuff/sleeve treatment was complete.
Bobbie Reynolds, El Cajon, CA

French Piping How-to

Here's how I make and insert French piping using either my conventional sewing machine or my serger.

First I mark the position for the piping on the wrong side of the fabric by pressing or finger-creasing the fabric. I fold the fabric, right sides together, along the marked line.

Then I prepare the piping by cutting a bias strip 1" (2.5 cm) wide and as long as needed for the finished piping. With right sides together, I fold the strip, meeting lengthwise edges, stitch along the lengthwise edge with a ⅛" (3-mm) seam to form a tube, and turn the tube right side out. I finger-press the piping flat, with the seamed edge along one pressed edge.

To insert the piping, I position the flat tubing with the seamed edge against the fold and pin in place. On a conventional sewing machine, I set the machine for a wide zigzag, loosen the upper tension, and attach an overcast guide foot or satin edge foot. Then I stitch so that only a few threads of the fold are caught by the zig of the stitch. The zag stitches pass over the foot.

Using a serger, I adjust the machine for a flatlock stitch with a wide stitch width and a long stitch length. I guide the fold under the presser foot so that only the edge of the fold is caught with the serger. Then I open the fabric flat and press.
Doris Shakley, Prescott Valley, AZ

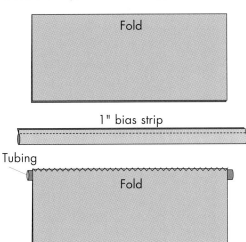

Fold

1" bias strip

Tubing

Fold

French Piping

Two-for-One Piping

I wanted to accent seams of a blouse with two rows of contrasting piping without having to spend time pinning, basting, and stitching each piece of piping individually. I joined the two piping pieces before inserting them into the garment. To do this I simply positioned the edge of the second piping so that it covered the stitching line of the first piping and stitched the two together using a zipper foot. It was easy to insert the combined piping into the garment.
Angela Bouck, Hudson, FL

Pintuck Foot Speeds Double Piping

When making a jacket with double piping on the collar and the sleeve cuffs, I found my 5-groove pintuck foot was just right for making the small piping and attaching the trim. The grooves held the piping in place perfectly as I stitched it to the garment. I used a glue stick to position the piping around the curves and walked the feet in this area. I've bought other sizes of pintuck feet to use on any piping I might decide to insert in the future. It's a breeze!
Sue Jones, Oklahoma City, OK

Recycle Dad's Ties

Strips cut from old ties make beautiful piping. Ties are often made of silk fabric, and since they are already cut on the bias, I can simply cut them from end to end. I just rip them open, cut lengths, get some cording, and make yards of piping. I use the piping to trim blouses, collars, jacket hems—any seam that looks good with piping. I use the small scraps remaining after I cut the strips to cover buttons for the garment.
Connie Castillo, Santa Ana, CA

Little Foot Has Big Uses

The Little Foot, sold primarily as a quilting foot, is wonderful for double topstitching on clothing (for example, down the front of a blouse or around sleeves).
Dolores Harrison, Yakima, WA

HEIRLOOM SEWING

Adding laces, pintucks, and trims to batiste and other fine fabrics is the hallmark of heirloom sewing. It's so much easier when you use these hints from "Sewing With Nancy" viewers!

Trim Your Lace Budget

To save money on beautiful eyelets and laces, I buy trims that can be cut in half lengthwise, so that I need only half of the yardage the pattern calls for!
Doris Hampton, Fort Smith, AR

Baby Slip at Baby Costs

My infant daughter needed a lace slip, but I preferred not to pay a lot. I used a size 3 months undershirt and sewed pink trim down the center front. Then I cut a 4½" x 28" (11.4-cm x 71.1-cm) strip of lace. I layered four rows of gathered lace onto the lace strip, sewed the strip, and then attached the lace strip to the shirt for a pretty (and inexpensive) slip.
Denise Bonecutter, Pt. Pleasant, WV

Baby Slip

Continuous Pintucks

To make rows and rows of pintucks, I sew them continuously in a tube to save time. I machine-baste together the top and the bottom of the fabric to be pintucked. Starting at the seam, I sew one row of pintucks. When I reach the beginning, I move the presser foot over so that the first pintuck falls in the groove of the foot and continue sewing in this way until all the rows are completed. All I have to do is cut the fabric apart at the basted seam.
Sharon Pultz, Clermont, FL

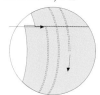

Pintucks in the Round

Note from Nancy

French hand sewing by machine is an heirloom sewing technique that combines ribbons, lace, and decorative stitchings to embellish classic garments. If you've never tried this type of sewing, you'll find that flannel is easier to handle for your first project than traditional lightweight fabrics such as batiste.

To create a simple yoke, combine ribbon, pintucks, puffing, and decorative machine stitches. Zigzag over the ribbon, creating colorful accents, and add rows of pintucks, using a pintuck sewing machine foot. The pintuck foot has ridges on the bottom to evenly space the rows. For a raised effect, place cording on the bottom of the foot. To puff an heirloom garment, gather along the edges of a fabric strip and sew the gathered strip onto the fabric yoke. Add decorative machine stitches as a finishing touch.

Polish Your Lace

To weave ribbon through lace, I use fingernail polish to stiffen the final ½" to ¾" (1.3 cm to 1.9 cm) of the ribbon. When dry, the ribbon easily weaves through the lace. I cut off the polished end when I'm finished.
Jean Hanson, Hawley, MN

Ripple-Free Ribbon

Before attaching ribbon to a garment, I first apply fusible web to the wrong side of the ribbon. I then fuse the ribbon to the garment, stitching it with monofilament thread. This prevents the wrinkles I used to get when stitching ribbon.
Wilodyne Bruce, Eau Claire, WI

Double Zigzag a Seam

When I want to join two pieces with finished edges, I butt them side by side with the right sides up (such as when joining two pieces of lace) and use a multiple zigzag stitch instead of the traditional zigzag stitch. I find that the smaller stitches make the stitching less visible, and it's easier to control the edges, especially when adding lace to a finished neckline or a collar edge. The finished joining is very flat.

Sometimes using a regular zigzag creates a ridge. That's an advantage in making a rolled edge, but when joining softer laces, I want them to remain perfectly flat. I could use spray starch, but that takes time. I am a real fan of methods such as this that do things easily, without requiring extra time.

Deb Cavanaugh, Spring Green, WI

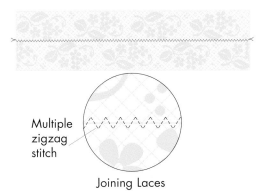

Multiple zigzag stitch

Joining Laces

Lace on Demand

My hint was born of sheer laziness. I hate with a passion to measure, to cut, and to pin trims to garments. Since I buy most trims by the yard for economic reasons, I store them on empty bathroom tissue tubes. Now when I want to add lace or some other trim to one of my daughter's garments, I put the trim tube on one of the spindles of my thread cone holder and place the cone holder on the floor near my machine. Then I run the trim to the machine bed and position it on top of the article to be embellished. Guiding it by hand as I sew, I let the trim feed off the roll as if it were thread. I no longer accidentally measure too much or too little trim or worry about excessive pinning on delicate fabrics.

Beverly Ayers, Kansas City, MO

"Heirloom" T-Shirts

I buy plain T-shirts in white, add a lace pocket and embellish the pocket with seed pearls, outlining each lace flower. I also use sequins and tiny satin flowers, stringing tiny silver beads to hang free from the centers of the flowers. It only takes ¼ yard (.23 m) to get started. I use the same technique on black T-shirts and have found that the pocket shows up better if I line it with a beige piece of leftover muslin.

Dolores Steiner, Huntingdon Valley, PA

Keep It Clean

When I made a bridal gown for my daughter, I wanted to add pearls and sequins to lace motifs but was concerned that I might soil the gown by handling it so much. I cut out all the lace motifs, added the pearls and the sequins, and then stitched the lace to the gown. The sections were so much easier to handle because they were smaller, and I didn't have the bulk or the weight of the gown to worry about.

Mary Rennich, Gloucester, VA

Ribbon Fabric

I create fabric from interwoven ribbons to add special accents to heirloom garments such as christening dresses. I use a piece of fusible interfacing slightly larger than the garment pattern piece as a backing. I position ribbons vertically on the interfacing, butting edges, and press-baste across the top. Then I weave rows of ribbon in and out horizontally through the vertical ribbons. I press to fuse the ribbons to the interfacing. I trace the garment pattern onto the ribbon, baste around the edges, and cut out the created fabric as desired.

Lynanne Berg, Poulsbo, WA

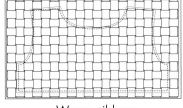

Woven ribbons

Perfect Marks

I mark the positions for laces, trims, or tucks on heirloom garments with my iron instead of a marking pen or pencil. Lines from marking pens or pencils are sometimes difficult to remove and may later reappear. By pressing to mark the positioning lines, I never need to worry about telltale lines that can identify a project as homemade.

Anne K. McGinley,
Las Cruces, NM

SPECIALIZED SEWING

Many of us have a favorite kind of stitching—
we love to make clothes, or we're avid
quilters, or we prefer to sew beautiful items
for our homes.

Most of the hints in the earlier chapters
were based on finding better, faster, and
easier ways to accomplish specific sewing
techniques or to use various sewing materials.
In this chapter we look at ways to come up
with better finished products. "Sewing With
Nancy" viewers have good ideas for making
clothing, creating gift items, sewing for home
decor, and quilting.

CLOTHING

Sew a collection of stylish accessories, transform adult wear into children's wear, or personalize ready-to-wear with these quick-and-easy hints.

Socks Lengthen Mittens

I often find that children's gloves or mittens are too short to fit their hands properly. I recycle children's old knee socks by cutting off the feet and then sewing the top parts to mittens and gloves. The extra length means no more cold wrists, and it's harder for my child to lose this unique handwear.

Katie Brandt,
St. Remy, NY

No-Slip Slip Belt

I like to wear slip belts (without eyelets), especially when I'm on a diet and my waistline is fluctuating. To keep the end of the belt from pulling out of the buckle, I add Velcro tape. I sew a 2" (5-cm) piece of the loop side to the underside of the belt overlap. I use a water-soluble marking pen to mark where the overlap fits now; I sew a 1" (2.5-cm) piece of the hook side at the mark. As I lose weight, I can tighten the belt as needed.

Karen Ferguson, Fay, OK

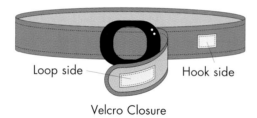

Loop side   Hook side

Velcro Closure

A Picture-Perfect Belt

A 5" x 45" (12.7-cm x 114.3-cm) fabric strip and a 47" (119.4-cm) length of picture hanging wire are all I need to make a belt to coordinate with my latest sewing project. (To adjust the length cut the picture wire to equal the length of the fabric plus 2" or 5 cm.)

I fold the fabric, with right sides together, raw edges aligned, and stitch a ¼" (6-mm) seam along the lengthwise edge and across one end. I fold under 1" (2.5 cm) at each end of the wire to form loops and secure the ends with tape. Then I hand-sew one of the loops to the end seam of the fabric, turn the fabric right side out over the wire and handstitch the other wire loop to the remaining end and stitch closed.

To wear the belt, I cross the belt ends in front and twist. Then I gather and crush the two belt ends to form a rosette.

Virgie LeBlue, Crowley, LA

Quick Patternless Dickeys

Cutting a dickey from an old blouse gave me a perfect accessory for little or no cost. I copied the dimensions for shoulder width and neck length from a purchased dickey. I found a good general guide is 12" (30.5 cm) from shoulder to the bottom and 4" (10 cm) from the neckline to the shoulder. I serged the cut edges, but I could also have sewn them on a machine with a zigzag stitch. I used the same technique to convert a knitted blouse into a turtleneck dickey.

Rita Zastrow, Aberdeen, WA

Dickey

Another idea: *Paula Gunn of Slidell, LA,* finds this a way to use blouses too good to discard but too snug to button comfortably. She says that she saved so much money, she went shopping!

A Scarf Secret

I fasten two safety pins on the inside of my jacket, placing one pin just above the buttons/buttonholes on each side. I drape a scarf around my neck and secure the ends by tucking them in the pins. The scarf hangs gracefully around my neck without slipping off, and I haven't put holes in delicate silk.

Marlene Fullmer, Chariton, IA

Bonny Bows

I was making a little girl's dress that had six bows. The pattern called for using 5⅛ yards (4.69 m) of 1½"-wide (3.8-cm-wide) ribbon. I decided to make bows from leftover fabric instead of buying ribbon.

For each bow, I cut a strip of fabric 18½" (47 cm) long and about 1¾" (4.4 cm) wide; then I cut a 1½" (3.8-cm) square for the center of each bow. I serged all edges with a narrow rolled hem. (On a conventional machine, I would use an overcast guide foot and a zigzag stitch.)

I marked the center of one long side and then marked the points halfway between the center and each end (creating quarter marks). I matched each quarter mark to the center and then folded each end to the center, forming four loops approximately 2" (5 cm) long. I wrapped thread around the middle of the bow, slightly drawing it in. Then I folded opposite sides of the square to the middle and wrapped the folded square around the middle of the bow. Hiding the seam on the back of the bow, I tacked the center in place. Using this technique assures that the right sides of the fabric is always visible.

Caroline McManis, Marion, IN

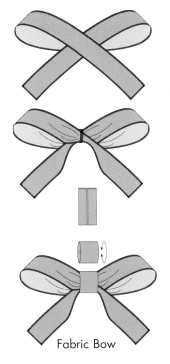

Fabric Bow

A Pocketful of Pretty

When I make decorative handkerchief-type inserts for pockets of silklike blouses, I sew the insert to two pieces of fusible interfacing, press the interfacing together, and cut the bottom of the interfacing to fit the pocket. The insert has no added bulk, and it conforms to the shape of my body.

Evelyn Turunen, Pelkie, MI

Other ideas: *Monica Barnhart of Leonore, IL,* simply rounds the bottom of a breast pocket (making it U-shaped instead of rectangular), pulls the lining up out of the pocket, and has a decorative, self-fabric pocket hanky. *Lorna Beverley of London, Ont., Canada* makes jacket pocket hankies from discarded neckties. For each hankie, she cuts off each end of a tie, making the two pieces about 1" (2.5 cm) longer than the amount she wants to show above the pocket. With the jacket on a flat surface, she puts the wide tie end into the pocket (point up) and places the narrow piece on top until she has an arrangement she likes. Then she bastes or fuses the tie ends together and stitches them to a piece of cardboard shaped to fit into the pocket.

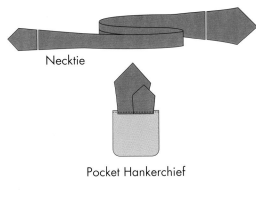

Necktie

Pocket Hankerchief

Thoughtful Turbans

When my mother lost her hair while undergoing chemotherapy, I designed a simple turban for her. My sewing guild now sews and donates turbans to local hospitals and to the American Cancer Society. Turbans are easy to make, look great as accessories with outfits, and are ego-boosters for cancer patients. We use woven, T-shirt, sweatshirt, or interlock scraps.

Rosemary Fajgier, Browns Mills, NJ

New Touches for Hand-me-downs

When I pass clothing down among my six daughters, I let the new wearer select new buttons, a bow, or an appliqué for the garment. Anything that helps the child focus on the fact that the article was individualized for her makes it easier to accept a hand-me-down.
Barbara Grimm,
LaCrosse, WI

Tablecloth Bibs

To make a quick gift for a baby shower, I purchase printed vinyl tablecloth fabric. Then I cut out a bib pattern and stitch bias tape around the edges, adding extra tape to make neck ties. I sew a small pocket at the bottom to catch crumbs. This fabric is wonderful for big spills, because the food mess doesn't leak through the bib and dampen the baby's clothing.
Cyndi Evans,
Sacramento, CA

Storing Pocket Hankies

Instead of storing my pocket inserts (hankies) in a cluttered drawer where they could get wrinkled, I keep them organized in my closet by using heavyweight interfacing to hold the hankies on a hanger. For each insert, I fuse together two layers of interfacing cut into the shape of the pocket. I fold and stitch the hankie to the interfacing and then punch a hole near the bottom of the insert with an ordinary paper punch. From one side of the interfacings, I cut a diagonal slit angled down into the punched hole. (This won't interfere with use.) Now I can hang many hankies upside down on a wire hanger, keeping them accessible and neat. I tie rubber bands approximately every inch (2.5 cm) on the hanger so that the inserts remain balanced and don't all slide to one side.
Sandra Mugridge, Allentown, PA

Interfacing

Pocket Hankerchief

Paint a Foot

Our son walked at nine months of age, when all his sleepers still fit. Since the sleepers were intended for infants who don't walk, they didn't have vinyl feet and the soles were very slick. I used dimensional paint pens to add designs on the feet and to provide enough traction to prevent falls. The same technique works for any footed garment.
Diane Williams, Liberty, MO

Custom Colors for a Jacket

My nine-year-old son Matthew wanted a neon-colored winter ski jacket. However I'd already taken advantage of a bargain on a solid blue, brand name jacket, and I wanted him to wear it. My solution was to add neon accents to the blue jacket. Matthew and I looked at several ski jackets in ready-to-wear catalogs to get color-blocking ideas and we decided to add a neon green upper collar and a neon green V design to the front of the coat.

Using green nylon fabric from my remnant box, I cut a piece to fit the shape of the top collar and pressed all edges under ¼" (6 mm). Then I simply topstitched the nylon onto the collar, gathering it slightly to fit around the neck, and replaced the jacket's hanger loop with a neon green one. For the front design, I cut out the two sides of the V separately, pressed under ¼" (6 mm), and then fused the pieces to the jacket just as I would an appliqué. The fusible web kept the pieces from shifting on the coat's slippery nylon outer shell while I topstitched the edges. It was surprisingly easy to stitch through all the layers of the coat. We were very pleased with the results—and with the money we saved!
Nancy Jepsen, Heppner, OR

A Scarf Is a Belt Is a Scarf

Out of a quarter of a yard of fabric (9" wide x 45" to 60" long or 22.9 cm x .23 m) I make scarves that I use as belts. After serging the edges (or turning under the edges and stitching conventionally), I weave the belt through three buckles, wrap it around my waist, and either tie the scarf in the back or loop the scarf ends through one of the belt buckles. The belt buckles are only attached to the scarf by weaving and can be removed for use with another scarf.
Sue Renner, Carlstadt, NJ

Scarf Belt

Recycle Dad's Wear for Daughter

To make a toddler's dress out of a man's shirt, I started with a basic unfitted dress pattern and one of my husband's unwanted shirts that was still in good condition. I removed the shirt's breast pocket and saved it to add to the skirt of the dress as an accent. The I centered the dress pattern front over the shirt's button area and cut it out, eliminating the need to sew buttons or buttonholes. I gathered the shirttail portion for the skirt of the dress, cut facings from the remaining shirt top and sleeve fabric, and constructed the dress according to the pattern instructions.
Loretta Woodall, Dallas, TX

Recycled Shirt

A Shirt Becomes a Dress

Using a child's sleeveless undershirt, I created a summer dress from scraps. First I removed the stitching from the undershirt's hem and added eyelet to the neckline and the arm-holes. Then I gathered a scrap of knit fabric and sewed it to the bottom of the undershirt. I used my serger to create a rolled hem, and my child had a cool, cute summer dress that was simple, inexpensive, and fast.
Teresa Lemkemann, E. Peoria, IL

More Coverage

Using one of my infant son's shirts as a pattern, I made a mealtime smock for him that covers his arms as well as his chest. The smock is basically a loose shirt worn backwards, with elastic cuffs and a Velcro tab at the back of the neck. I sewed three smocks so that I have a clean, dry one for each meal of the day.
Jeanie Chibbaro, Lanham, MD

Dusty Pants

When children's jogging pants become worn at the knees, I cut the pants off to make shorts. From each leftover pant leg, I make a dust cloth or a mitt for washing the car. I sew up the cut end, leaving the ribbing at the other end intact to hold the mitt snug against my wrist. From larger leftover leg pieces cut from adult jogging pants, I make bags to store my shorts when traveling.
Bev Gariepy,
Vancier City, Ont.,
Canada

Pouf Socks from Scraps

I use scraps from outfits that I've made for my little girls to create coordinating pairs of pouf socks.

For each sock, I cut off 1½" (3.8 cm) from the top of the sock (or cut directly below the tighter ribbed area). I cut a 1½" x 10" (3.8-cm x 25.4-cm) fabric strip and sew the short ends together, forming a tube. With right sides together, I pin the tube to the sock, stretching the sock to meet the tube, and sew or serge the two layers together with a ¼" (6-mm) seam. I repeat at the top of the tube, joining the ribbing section to the fabric tube.
Mary Newman, Chicago, IL

Personal Accessories and Gifts

"Sewing With Nancy" viewers know lots of clever ways to sew items for gift-giving, storing jewelry, and more.

Pendant Jewelry

I made a hanger for lapel pins and scatter pins so that I can easily see them without searching through a drawer or a jewelry box. I cut two pieces of single-faced quilted fabric to fit a wooden hanger and then serged together the tops and the sides, leaving an opening for the hook. I simply pin the jewelry to the quilted fabric.
Karlene Davis, Muskogee, OK

Spray Your Bows

I make hair bows for my daughter by hot-gluing ribbon or brightly colored shoelace bows onto metal barrettes. (Grosgrain ribbon works much better than satin ribbon.) I spray each finished bow with hair spray to give it extra body and to help it hold its shape.
Mary Jo Wippold, St. Louis, MO

Make Buttons into Earrings

Several friends and I convert buttons into custom jewelry. We snap the shank off a plastic button using a pair of pliers or nail clippers and then glue the button onto an earring post (available at crafts stores). We glue a larger version of the same button to a pin back to make a matching pin. For buttons with gold metallic paint, we spray on a sealer to prevent tarnishing. We recycle buttons without shanks by gluing faceted flat-backed faux jewels onto the front of each (over the holes) before adding posts to the backs.
Jane DeZearn, Talbott, TN

A Fabric Farm

Using fabric with motifs appropriate for children (such as farm animals or vehicles) I make a learning toy for children. I buy enough fabric to cut out each motif plus a 36" (91.4-cm) square. I fuse interfacing to the back of the fabric to stiffen it, cut out the square, and then cut out each motif from the leftover fabric. Children match each cutout to the motif on the square, saying the motif's name and making its sound (if appropriate).
Patricia Techlin, Appleton, WI

Double Wedding Gifts

At a bridal shower that my daughter's godmother gave for her, the guests were asked to wrap their gifts with something that the bride could use rather than with paper and ribbons. The many imaginative gift wraps included hand-embroidered tea towels, bath towels, and cleaning rags. One young woman wrapped her gift in a T-shirt and used a ponytail scrunchie for the bow. I basted four napkins together and made a scrubber pom-pom from nylon net for the bow.
Janice Beitz, Fort Collins, CO

Hypoallergenic Baby Wipes

Disposable diaper wipes containing alcohol irritated my nephew's skin, so I got out my 100%-cotton scraps (left over from various projects) and serged a stack of washable wipes. Using a wide 3/4-thread stitch to withstand numerous washings, I can either draw a pattern onto a scrap before serging or use the scrap in its existing shape. Small square scraps (8" to 10" or 20.3 cm to 25.4 cm) were perfect when he was a newborn; I increased the size to 12" (30.5 cm) or more as he grew. These wipes are easy to distinguish from faceclothes and are good for the environment.
Theresa Frank, Aurora, CO

Bag Your Vitamins

Packing for a vacation, I created a carrier for vitamins and medications so that I wouldn't have to carry all the bottles. I sewed four compartments from top to bottom on a large zip-top plastic bag and then filled each with one day's pills. Then I sewed a horizontal seam enclosing the pills. I filled four more days' worth and enclosed them, repeating the process until I had a compartment for each day of my vacation. To use, I simply snipped one compartment each day as needed.
Linda Hall, Stockton, MO

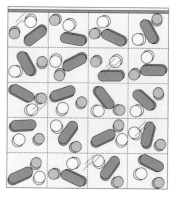

Travel Pill Organizer

Keep Silver Baubles Shiny

To keep sterling earrings, necklaces, and pins tarnish free, I make jewelry bags out of an antitarnish cloth such as Atlantic Cloth. I've made jewelry bags with zippers or drawstring closures to hold single pieces of jewelry, and I've also made pouches with several compartments to hold multiple items.

I cut a 10"-diameter (25.4-cm-diameter) circle and a 6"-diameter (15.2-cm-diameter) circle out of antitarnish cloth. I clean-finish the edge of the smaller circle and center it on the larger. I stitch from edge to edge to divide the smaller circle into six or eight pie-shaped wedges.

I bind the edge of the larger circle with bias tape, leaving openings at opposite sides of the circle, and then insert a cord through each opening. To close the pouch, I pull both cords.
Cindy Beske, Anniston, AL

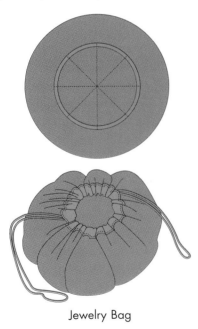

Jewelry Bag

Note from Nancy

Atlantic Cloth, a softly napped 100%-cotton fabric available from Nancy's Notions and sewing centers, has a special finish that keeps out tarnish-causing gases. You won't have to spend hours polishing your jewelry or silver pieces when they're stored in cases made from this fabric!

A Place for Everything

To keep my family organized when we play a board game, I made a storage pocket for each player to hold cards, money, tokens, or other game pieces. For each pocket, I cut a rectangle of clear plastic twice as long as I wanted the finished pocket to be and then folded it so that one short edge extended 2" to 4" (5.1 cm to 10.2 cm) above the other edge. Then I stitched both side seams. Now it's easy to set the game aside for interruptions such as meals.
Jane Easton, West Union, IA

Accessorize with Leftovers

When I have to shorten a ready-to-wear garment, I use the portion cut off at the hem to make a matching fabric flower pin. I've also made these flowers from scraps left over from sewing projects.

I decide how wide I want the flower to be and cut a fabric strip twice that width. With wrong sides together, I fold the strip in half lengthwise, machine-baste along the cut edges, and then pull the basting threads to gather the strip. I roll the gathered strip into the shape of a flower and hot-glue the gathered side to a purchased pin back from a crafts store. Sometimes I attach a covered button, beads, or sequins at the center and add leaves cut from nonraveling green fabric.
Cheryl Fowler, Ft. Oglethorpe, GA

Moths, Begone!

Finding a moth-eaten sweater inspired me to start making antimoth sachets for myself and for inexpensive Christmas gifts. I use two 4" (12.2-cm) squares of leftover fabric filled with inexpensive cedar chips available at pet stores. With right sides together and raw edges aligned, I stitch three sides of the squares, turn the fabric right side out, fill the sachet with chips, and then sew the fourth side. For gift-giving, I embellish the fabric first with decorative stitches and appliqués. (I've used lace as the base fabric, but chips tend to poke through and could snag the stored woolens.)
Judy Mackey, Fort Worth, TX

Save Extra Invitations

Like most new brides, I had quite a few wedding invitations left over. I tore off the backs, sewed a design around the edges, and used them as thank-you notes.
Cathy Grant,
Seattle, WA

Memories in a Box

Using fabric left over from the bridesmaids' dresses, I covered a heart-shaped box to hold wedding cards from my son and daughter-in-law's wedding.
Marion Gade,
Fox Lake, WI

Memory Box

HOME DECOR

Dress up any room in your house and make practical kitchen and bath accessories using these helpful hints.

Make a Manual Lettuce Spinner

Here's a funny idea I call a manual lettuce spin dryer. I make a muslin bag (approximate finished size is 12" x 26" or 30.5 cm x 66 cm) using prewashed muslin. I insert washed lettuce and spin— preferably outdoors! Salad greens come out dry, and the bag is less expensive than the ones available in gourmet stores. Claudia DeCosta, Yampa, CO

Save a Towel

For towels that are still in good condition except that the edges are frayed or worn, I create new edges and salvage those towels for more use. I serge the edges, adjusting to make the stitches as close together as possible and letting the serger trim the frayed edges. I can turn under the new edges and hem them on a conventional sewing machine or leave the serged edges as is, if they seem secure enough to withstand multiple washings. Then I add whatever lace, ribbon, or other trim I like onto one end. I press to get a professional finish, and I have a towel with a completely different look. *Cheryl Radley, Des Moines, WA*

Elasticize a Bed Skirt

When making a bed skirt for a redecorated bedroom, I used clear elastic to gather the fabric. I measured the three sides of my bed and doubled that measurement to determine the length I needed for the fabric strip. Then I cut a piece of clear elastic to equal the length of the original measurement, stretched it to fit the flat fabric strip, and sewed it in place. Using clear elastic took less time than conventional gathering techniques, I didn't have to worry about broken basting threads, and my gathers came out even. To make the skirt reversible, I stitched the existing bedskirt on top of the new bed skirt, with the wrong sides together. *Marjorie Latimer, Burlington, Ont., Canada*

Economy Pillowcases

I use king-size pillows on my twin beds. Since I often find twin sheets on sale without any matching king-size pillowcases, I buy an extra twin sheet (flat or fitted) to make pillowcases and use the remaining fabric to decorate towels for the adjoining bathroom. *Laura Neal, Orlando, FL*

Pockets Hold Pillows

At a bridal shower more than 30 years ago, I received pillowcases with pockets to prevent the pillows from sliding out of the cases. They worked so well that I've been making them ever since.

I cut two rectangular pieces for each pillowcase, making one rectangle 6" (15.2 cm) longer than the other. For standard pillows, I cut one rectangle 21" x 34" (53.3 cm x 86.4 cm) and the other 21" x 40" (53.3 cm x 101.6 cm). On the small rectangle, I turn one short edge under ½" (1.3 cm) and press; then I turn under a 3" (7.6-cm) hem and stitch. On the large rectangle, I turn one short edge under ½" (1.3 cm) and press; then I turn under another ½" (1.3 cm) and stitch.

I meet the unstitched short edges of the rectangles, with the right sides together, and sew a ½" (1.3-cm) seam. I fold the extension of the larger rectangle over the hem of the smaller rectangle and stitch ½" (1.3-cm) side seams. When I turn the extension right side out, a pocket forms that holds the pillow in place. Then I turn the entire pillowcase right side out. *Ricki Buryta, Stoney Creek, Ont., Canada*

Pillowcase

Recycled Scrubbers

I remove the paper label and metal grommet from two fruit or vegetable plastic mesh bags and flatten them with a book for a few days. Next, I place the bags atop each other, fold the ends toward the middle, and then fold them in half. I stitch the three open sides together using a wide zigzag stitch. Voilà, I have a free scrubber.
Margie Seefeld, Laurel, MS

Stuff Those Toys

My three children have many stuffed toys. To store the toys, I made an over-the-door stuffed toy holder. I cut a piece of stretchy, meshlike fabric a little smaller than the dimensions of the door.

To make the pocket for the door top, I serged the top edge, folded it down 6" (15.2-cm), added a tuck to allow for the door's thickness and then serged both sides. Although my children keep their door open, the fabric is thin enough that it shouldn't interfere with closing the door.

I hemmed each pocket and inserted elastic to hold the toys in place. I made a gusset in the bottom, and stitched the pocket to the base of the fabric. To keep the holder from curling forward when it hangs, I stitched a bias tape casing above each pocket and added a loop at the outer edges of each pocket.

Then I topstitched straight grain binding to the outer edges using a conventional sewing machine; inserted a small dowel into each casing through the back; and laced a cord through the loops and across the back of the door.
Masha Fontes, Ithaca, NY

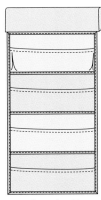

Pockets for Toys

From Sofa to Table

I make table linens out of upholstery fabric. I can cut nine 13" x 18" (33-cm x 47.7-cm) place mats from a little more than 1 yard (91.4 cm) of fabric. I thread my serger's upper looper with pearl cotton and decrease the stitch width so that I get a covered look on the finished edges.

From leftover fabric, I cut nine 1½" x 5" (3.8-cm x 12.7-cm) napkin holders. I finish the edges of these using a narrow serger stitch and pearl cotton in the upper looper. Then I overlap the ends ⅜" (1 cm) and stitch with a conventional machine.
Lori Owen, Vancouver, BC, Canada

Note from Nancy

What a great idea! Always prewash the fabric to make sure it can take the repeated washing and drying that place mats get. I like to round the corners of the mats to make it easier to serge the edges.

No Flying Tablecloths

To keep a patio tablecloth from blowing away, sew four small bags from the same fabric as the tablecloth and fill them about three-quarters full of sand. Sew the top of each bag shut and stitch a buttonhole. Then sew pretty buttons on each corner of the tablecloth. Button the little bags on to hold the cloth in place and unbutton and remove them to launder the cloth.

Another technique for anchoring outdoor tablecloths is to attach a small pocket on the wrong side of each corner at the hem edge. Then simply place a rock or other small, heavy object into each pocket to keep the cloth in place.
Helga G. Koehler, Slinger, WI, and Betty McKinney, Belen, NM

Make Tablecloths into Napkins

I have several of my mother's linen tablecloths that are wearing out, so I use the good parts to make napkins. I cut them in the size I need and finish the edges with a decorative serger overlock stitch or a serged rolled hem, using thread that matches or coordinates with my china.
Ellen Derksen,
Waupun, WI

Plump Your Pillows

My father, who was an upholstery instructor, taught me to cut the outside cover for pillows slighter smaller than the pillow insert. This method makes a plumper pillow.
Lillian Laack, Sheboygan, WI

Keep Recipe Cards Clean

Make recipe card protectors out of clear vinyl yardage, cut into 5" x 7" (12.7-cm x 17.8-cm) pieces with an office-type paper cutter. (You could use a rotary cutter and mat.) Sew two pieces together across the top only, and you have a cover that keeps a recipe clean even during cooking. You can also flip the covered card over and continue reading on the back.
Donna Cole, Akron, OH

Chocolate Chip Cookies

1 Cup Butter	1 Tsp Salt
3/4 Cup Sugar	2 Cups Flour
3/4 Cup Brown Sugar	1 Tsp. Vanilla
2 Eggs	12 Oz Pkg. Chocolate Chips
1 Tsp Baking Soda	1/2 Cup Nuts

Preheat oven to 350°. Sift dry ingredients. Cream butter, sugar, and brown sugar. Blend in dry ingredients and add vanilla. Stir in chocolate chips and nuts. Place by teaspoonful on cookie sheets and bake for 12 to 15 minutes.

Recipe Card Protector

A Pillow with a Handle

I make it easy for my children to take their favorite pillows wherever they go by adding handles to the pillow covers. I start with an inexpensive polyester-filled pillow and cover the pillow with a sturdy material such as denim or washable drapery fabric. I insert a suitcase-style handle into the seam at one end and put a zipper or hook-and-loop tape into the other seam so that the cover is easy to remove and launder.
Mickey Smith, Pine Bluffs, WY

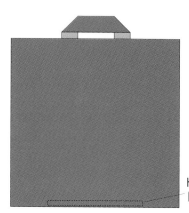

Hook-and-loop tape

Pillow Cover

Snuggly, Nonslip Duvet Cover

I made a duvet cover to coordinate with a newly decorated bedroom. The top of the duvet was a fashion sheet, and the bottom was a flannel sheet. I chose a flannel sheet for the underside because I thought it would be warm and snuggly. The bonus was that the flannel sheet keeps the comforter from moving around inside the duvet.
Heather Browning, Long Beach, CA

Lumpless Pillows

This past year I made several pillows and was unhappy with the corners and the general lumpiness of the stuffing. So now I cut a piece of batting equal in size to my pillow fabric and treat the fabric and the batting as one while sewing. I place the batting on the wrong side of the pillow fabric and stitch the layers together using a wide, long zigzag stitch. This stabilizes the batting and joins the layers where the opening for turning will be.

Then I place the right sides of the pillow fabric together, matching the zigzagged ends, and stitch the side seams using a ¼" (6-mm) seam allowance. I stitch a short distance from each corner on the zigzagged end, using a ½" (1.3-cm) seam allowance and leaving an opening for turning.

When I turn the pillow right side out I find that my pillow has well-defined corners and a smooth surface. I stuff the pillow as desired and slipstitch the opening closed.
Linda Simonson, Cass Lake, MN

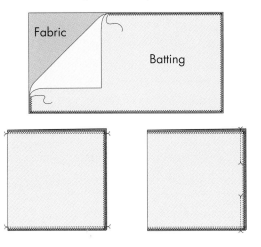

Pillow Fabric

Another idea: *Mary Wood of Bramalea, Ont., Canada*, leaves the batting in the seam allowance (no grading of the seam allowance), and when she turns the work to the right side before stuffing, she topstitches a narrow border all around to give the appearance of cording. To imitate a wider rolled edge, she cuts the batting wider all around and topstitches a wider border, enclosing the extra batting.

Cushions with Meaning

For padded cushions that tie onto chairs, I've had to resew the ties many times because they tear off quite easily. I overcame this by stitching a doubled piece of ¼"-wide (6-mm-wide) elastic in a loop where each tie would usually be inserted. (Doubling the elastic provides extra strength.) Then I made spaghetti ties, put the ties through the elastic loops, and tied the cushion to the back of the chair. This gives the cushion a bit of ease so that the ties don't tear off.
Marion Robson, Peterborough, Ont., Canada

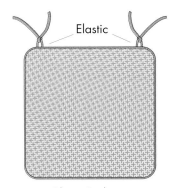

Chair Cushion

Iron a Straight Line

I found it difficult to measure and sew a straight line for a curtain rod pocket. Now I measure once and use my iron to mark the stitching line. I use a 3" (7.6-cm) heading and a 3" (7.6-cm) rod pocket when I make country curtains. Here's what I do:

I finish the cut edge by serging, zigzagging, or pressing under ¼" (6 mm), and then I press under a 6" (15.2-cm) hem and stitch. I meet the top edge to the stitched hem edge and press. The crease is my sewing guide for the second line of stitching. I use this method on anything that has a heading or a casing. It's faster than measuring and marking both lines.
Beulah Frazier, Saint Albans, WV

Stitching Guide Lines

Tips for a Tablecloth

I appliquéd a tablecloth for a friend, cutting the cloth from a pastel flat sheet so that I'd have an unseamed piece of fabric. Next I machine-appliquéd the cloth. I finished the edges by using a serged rolled hem with slightly darker thread than the cloth. Then I zigzagged lace to the wrong side of the edge with a conventional sewing machine. The effect was striking!
N. Lorena Martin,
Ft. Huachuca, AZ

Stuff the Corners

I often have trouble making the polyester stuffing stay in the corners of pillows. Now I stitch a piece of fiberfill into each corner as I sew the pillow's seams. When I turn the pillow right side out, the filler stays in place.
Shirley Stumpf,
Indianapolis, IN

Timesaving Sponges

I am not only a sewer but also a nurse anesthetist, wife, and mother. A more efficient sponge gets my cleaning done faster so that I can go back to sewing. I buy the least expensive sponges I can find and cover them with nylon net and terry cloth scraps. I cut the fabric pieces slightly larger than the sponge, sandwich the sponge in between a terry cloth piece and a nylon net piece, and then use my serger to stitch the fabrics together. (If you don't have a serger, zigzag the layers together.) The nylon net is a good scrubber, and the terry side is great for wiping up.
Cindy Konchanin, Sayre, PA

Clothespins Hold Draperies

Since the fabric I use for pleated draperies is very thick, it's hard to pin the pleats in place. I use clothespins instead. If the pleats don't work out right the first time I fold them, it's easy to unpin and redo them. I also find clothespins handy when I hem heavy fabrics such as denim or raincoat vinyl.
Kay Weslow, Frostburg, MD

Money-Saving Curtain Rods

Instead of buying 2" (5.1-cm) and 4" (10.2-cm) curtain rods, make them by adding rod inserts cut from cardboard or firm plastic to conventional 1" (2.5-cm) rods. Cut the cardboard or plastic in the desired width (for example, 2" or 5.1 cm) and then cut the desired total length of the rod, including returns. Slip the rod insert into the casing, thread the 1" (2.5-cm) rod behind the insert in the casing, and mount the rod as usual. The insert holds up well, saves the expense of purchasing new rods, and recycles old rods when you sew new window treatments.
Cynthia Johnson, Kaysville, UT, and Dorothy Lindstrom, Auburn, CA

Bag a Balloon Curtain

My neighbor and I agree that the perfect stuffing for pouf curtains is plastic grocery bags. These bags weigh less than tissue paper, and they seem to hold their shape better. The best part is that I'm recycling when I use them.
Jan Baker, Temple Terrace, FL
Another idea: *Irma Saarnio of Hudson, FL,* uses air—she places zip-top plastic bags in her pouf valances or curtains and fills them with the amount of air she needs to achieve the look she wants.

Three-for-One Pleats

To make old-fashioned pinch-pleated draperies (no pleating tape), I sew the seam to make a 5" (12.7-cm) pleat, and then I stitch another seam ⅝" (1.6 cm) from the edge. This becomes my middle pleat. I press the folded edge, refold, and press so that the seam of the middle pleat is centered atop the first seam. I have three perfect pleats!
Elaine Coniglio, Tampa, FL

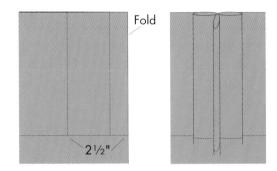

Pinch Pleats

Curtained Storage

Our new home's kitchen has about a 10" (25.4-cm) space between the cabinets and the ceiling that I needed to use to store large appliances, such as a popcorn popper and a wok. I sewed a small valance using my kitchen curtain fabric. My husband attached 1" x 2" (2.5-cm x 5.1-cm) strips of wood to the ceiling, and then we used a staple gun to attach the valance.
Sharolyn Blume, Pleasant Grove, UT

Keep Costs out of the Clouds

I recently made 20 cloud valances for our windows. Trying to keep costs down, I eliminated the loop shade tape called for in the instructions. Instead, I bar-tacked over the cording at regular intervals, pulled up the curtain until I achieved the desired effect, and tied the cords. I used little cording and saved a lot on tape.
Angie Pellmann, Millstadt, IL

Note from Nancy

It takes a little time to measure and mark the positions for the bar-tacking on the valances so that the bar tacks are evenly positioned throughout the valance. And be sure you stitch *over* rather than through the cording, or you won't be able to pull up the cords.

Bed in a Bag

When redecorating my bedroom, I tried to do it within a budget. I purchased on sale a queen-size "Bed in a Bag" set, consisting of a comforter, dust ruffle, shams, sheets, and pillowcases. I made curtains for the two windows from the sheets. When I tried but failed to find some lace trim to match the bone background of the curtains, my solution was to purchase white trim and soak it in weak tea until I got the desired shade.
Gloria Kruft, Baltimore, MD

Fusing Dinosaurs

When my three-year-old moved out of the nursery into his "big boy" room, I wanted to decorate in dinosaurs but was surprised at the cost of ready-made decorations. I couldn't see spending a lot of money on things he would outgrow. I found a remnant of dinosaur fabric, fused it to cardboard, and cut out the animals. I attached the dinosaurs to the wall using carpet tape. (My son enjoyed peeling off the paper backing.) The shapes are easily removed, and the carpet tape doesn't hurt the walls. My son uses his wall as a big felt board!
Gayle Case, San Diego, CA

The Perfect Storage Holder

Twenty years ago I saw a clever display of potholders that sparked my imagination. I designed a holder that can be hung just about anywhere storage is needed. This holder makes a wonderful gift for the person who has everything.

Pad a piece of ¼" (6-mm) or ½" (1.3-cm) plywood with batting; cover tightly with firm fabric. (I prefer solid colored, tweedy upholstery fabrics for the covering, since they're durable, easy to clean, and don't show pin marks.) Hang the piece up and insert drapery hooks upside down wherever you wish. To place the hooks in a straight line, pin a tape measure to the board as you insert the hooks.
Ruth Eggleston, Sparks, NV

Nancy's Notions Box

I covered a box with cutouts from an expired Nancy's Notions *catalog. It makes a great treasure box, sewing box, travel sewing kit, or whatever you wish it to be. It's also great for storing tiny items.*
Burnice Octabienski, Hamilton., Ont., Canada

Instant Valances

Choose a napkin. Add tassels at the corners if you like. Fold it in half diagonally and position it over a curtain rod or a dowel. Use one or a series of napkins across a window. It's *so* easy! You can change your window treatment whenever you want!
Gail Brown, Hoquiam, WA

Note from Nancy

Gail Brown, author of *Instant Interiors*, likes using shortcuts in home decorating. Her tips are practical, smart, and money wise.

Sporty Sheets

When I want to make or alter fitted sheets, I use Sew Through Sport Elastic at the corners. I just fold the elastic in half lengthwise, encase the corner of the sheet with the folded elastic, and stitch, stretching the elastic to fit. I use the same technique for stool and chair covers.
Liz Barefoot, Bonifay, FL

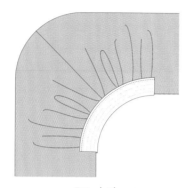

Fitted Sheet

Turn Arm Covers into Pillows

I wanted to make new throw pillows for our couch but couldn't find a printed fabric that looked right with the couch's upholstery, so I used the arm covers that came with the couch (those pesky little pieces of fabric that were always out of place, usually stuffed into the ends of the couch). After taking out hems, the arm covers were perfect 16" (40.6-cm) squares. I used these as the pillow fronts and made piping, ruffles, and backs out of a coordinating solid fabric. They turned out so well many of my friends thought they came with the couch.
Joyce J. Miller, Chillicothe, OH

Turn Towels into Curtains

To spruce up my bathroom inexpensively whenever I want, I make quick curtains from two bath towels. First, I measure the length of the window to determine how long the curtains must be. Then, with the right side of a towel facing me, I fold one of the fringed or embellished ends towards me to give the illusion of a valance and sew it in place, using a seam allowance wide enough to accommodate the curtain rod. I repeat the process on the other towel. If I'm using plain towels, I dress up the curtains using leftover trim or lace. When I'm tired of the curtains, I just remove the stitching and use the towels for bathing.
Donna Lincecum, Riddle, OR

Towel Curtains

Serging Selvages

We recently moved and I found myself faced with a whole house of window treatment sewing. Cutting the selvages from the fabrics with a rotary cutter got to be a tedious job. I took the thread and the needle out of my serger and ran the fabric through, letting the knife cut the selvage from the fabric. I had a clean cut with a straight edge.
Betty Farrell, Mobile, AL

Serge King-size Batting

When I must sew large pieces of batting together to use in king-size bedding, I join the pieces using my serger's flatlock stitch. This technique leaves the batting very smooth so that there's no indentation at the seam when I cover it with fabric. Serging the seam is so much faster than feather-stitching it by hand.
Teri Dyer, Denton, TX

Bonus Baby Blankets

I purchased a soft, full-size blanket, cut it into four pieces, and bound the edges of each piece using a baby fabric print that I had cut on the bias. This technique gave me four baby gifts from one purchase.
Evelyn Partlow, Pickerington, OH

Make a Memory Pillow

My late husband's neckties were too nice to discard, so I combined pieces of the fabrics to create a memory —a minipillow. I've made seven of these little pillows for family members.
Gertrude Lovig, McGregor, IA

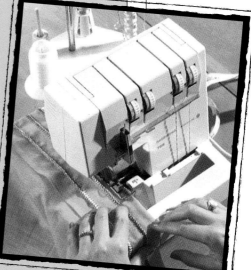

The Serger Changed Sewing

Many years ago when I pulled my mail-order serger out of the box, I stared at it with the same wonder I still have when I look under my car's hood. After a 45-minute threading ordeal, I managed to serge an overlock stitch and thought, "Why did I order this?" Then I decided to read the instructions!

The serger was the first catalyst for transporting sewing enthusiasts into high-tech sewing. Clean-finishing edges at 1500 stitches per minute or serging a T-shirt in 30 minutes or less gave us an entirely new perspective on sewing.

In addition, the serger's embellishment options with decorative threads took serged seams beyond basic to creative. With the frequent introduction of new serger threads, notions, ribbons, and machine improvements, the creative options seem to be practically limitless.

Sergers really changed my way of sewing and have proven to be a vehicle to attract a whole new generation to the creative art of sewing. As one preteen in a recent sewing class stated, "I'd rather serge than watch 'Nick at Night!'"

QUILTING

Some sewers would say we've saved the best for last—a host of hints on designing, making, and finishing quilts.

Machine Quilt Tying

I have arthritis, which sometimes makes hand-tying a quilt difficult. Instead I adjust my sewing machine as if I were going to sew on a button and then stitch wherever I would ordinarily tie the quilt. I make the stitches a little longer for a large quilt and can finish the entire quilt this way.
Alice Maliongas, Hampton, VA

A Quick Quilt Cover-up

Sometimes my quilt backing shrinks 1" or 2" (2.5 cm or 5.1 cm) after being machine-quilted. When this common problem happens, I cut my binding wide enough to cover the difference and apply the binding. In most cases it adds to the beauty of my piece.
Rose Chye, Custer, MI

Make a Square Square

I'm making a wall hanging using many different jewel-tone prints. I cut the fabric pieces into squares, divided the squares into triangles, and seamed the bias edges of two different pieces.

The bias stretches easily, so I took pieces of ThreadFuse and placed them on the right side of one of the triangles, within the bias seam allowance. I carefully positioned the second bias triangle over the first, with right sides together, and pressed. The pieces do not stretch, so the pieced square turns out square!
Marie Beachy, Sarasota, FL

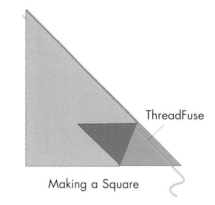

Making a Square

No More Wobbly Wedges

I needed to cut 80 wedges, and I didn't want the wedge ruler to slip, so I turned to water-soluble basting tape. I put the tape on the ruler back; the tape was sticky enough to be lifted off the fabric 80 times and put back down in a new position. When I was through, I washed the ruler and the tape dissolved.
Cathy Grant, Seattle, WA

Fuse Binding in Place

Once I've finished quilting or tying a project, I stitch the binding to the quilt's raw edge with ThreadFuse in my bobbin. I sew the quilt and the binding together so that the fusible thread is on top of the quilt. Then I bring my binding around to the top of the quilt, and instead of pinning, I use my iron. After the binding is fused to the quilt, I can either handstitch or machine-stitch around the edge without having pins stick me or fall out.
Kim Anderson, White Bear Lake, MN

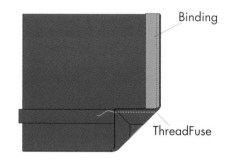

Binding

ThreadFuse

Adding Binding

Bag a Quilt

To keep quilts clean while I work on them, I made a big bag from a single flat sheet, folding the sheet in half and sewing the sides. To use the bag, I put it on the floor, stand my quilt in its frame or hoop in the center of the bag, and tuck the quilt inside the bag. I work on the quilt by sitting halfway into the bag (shoes off, of course). When I'm finished quilting for the day or if company's coming, I pull up the sides of the bag, enclosing the quilt, and use clothespins to secure the top. I can easily store the quilt until the next time I'm ready to work on it.
Gig Busch, Dade City, FL

Expand Fabric Options

In quilting projects (especially wall hangings) I often want to use a fabric that has a particular color, sheen, texture, or pattern that is only available in a lightweight fashion fabric. These types of fabrics don't hold their shape well during construction or in the finished product, and it's hard to cut out small pieces accurately.

I tried using starch to add body, but that wasn't a good solution. I've found that using a lightweight fusible interfacing works very well. I apply the interfacing to the needed amount of fabric, and then I can cut and sew my pieces accurately. The interfacing makes it easy to mark sewing lines, and these interfaced pieces retain their shape very well in the finished project.
Françoise Calvin, Fairview Heights, IL

A Gripping Hint

My main sewing projects are now quilts—all machine-pieced but hand-quilted, from miniature to king-size. In order to obtain small quilting stitches, I use a size 10 between needle.

I sometimes had difficulty gripping the needle to pull it through the fabrics. I went to an office supply store and purchased a rubber finger (usually used to help turn pages or count money). I found that if I cut it so that it just reaches my first finger joint, it fits very comfortably and is always there to help pull the needle through.

When my sister started quilting recently, she couldn't use the small needles because of arthritis. I gave her a rubber finger, and now she can use and grasp the smaller needle.
Helen Miller, Waupaca, WI

Legible Labels

I love to quilt, but adding labels was a chore until I discovered that I could type my labels on cloth and then hand stitch them to the back of the quilt. By typing them I could include any necessary information.
Shirley Andrews, Peoria, IL

Make Stitching in-the-Ditch Easier

When stitching in-the-ditch (stitching in the well of the seam from the right side of the fabric to make the stitching virtually invisible), I need to gently ease the two fabric sections apart to prevent catching the edges of the fabrics in the stitching. Because I often use smooth cottons for quilts, I find it difficult to get a good grip on the fabric to ease the sections apart. I buy rubber fingers from a stationery store and put them on the fingers I use to pull the fabrics apart.
Hannah MacLeod, Calgary, Alta., Canada

Cook Up a Quilt Design

Recently I wanted to embellish the borders of miniquilts using seasonal patterns; I didn't have any stencils, so I used cookie cutters to create my quilting designs. I rubbed chalk along the lower edge of each cookie cutter to outline the edge and then stamped each quilt. The designs lasted just long enough for me to machine-quilt them. I used stars, bells, and angels for these Christmas quilts; I have other cookie cutters in shapes that will work well for other holidays projects and for baby quilts.
Lori Clausen, Lindsay, NE

An Improvisation

One day while watching "Sewing With Nancy" and quilting at the same time, I needed to find something to remove chalk lines from my quilt top, but I didn't want to miss part of the show. So I tore off a small scrap of polyester batting, held the quilt firmly over my knee, and rubbed with the batting scrap. It worked beautifully.
Vivian Krebs,
Houston, TX

Jeans Quilts

I save old jeans and then cut and piece them to make quilts for teenagers (boys and girls). I also make pillows to match. Denim jeans seem to have endless colors and fabric textures.
Joan Loeffelholz, Waunakee, WI

Quick Organizers

After I cut all the pieces for a quilting square, I place a bath towel on my cutting table and arrange the pieces in the pattern I've chosen. If necessary, I layer several towels in the same fashion. I simply roll up the towels and carry them to the sewing machine, carefully unrolling them on the open leaf of the machine table. Then I'm ready to stitch. I can also tidy up and quickly put the strips away until later if my sewing is interrupted.
Gerri Johnston, Pittsburgh, PA

Other ideas: *Becky Cauble of Charlotte, NC,* sorts quilt strips in cutlery trays, either by color or by the sequence in which they will be used. *Pat Byrnes of Port Richey, FL,* organizes strips on hangers using clothespins to attach the strips in the order that she'll need to sew them. *Robbins E. Rice of Melbourne, FL,* made an organizer from thin wood paneling, assembling the various bins with a hot-glue gun.

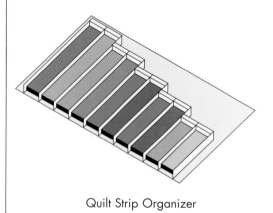

Quilt Strip Organizer

Chart Your Quilt

When I make a quilt, I prepare a chart of the fabric swatches. When I finish the quilt, I place the chart plus pieces of each fabric (for possible future repairs) in a zip-top plastic bag. I try to include a 4" or 5" (10.2-cm or 12.7-cm) square of each fabric. If I give the quilt away, I include the mending pieces and the chart.
Marlene May, North Fort Meyers, FL

Use Prequilted Lining

When I need to quilt a fabric—and added fabric body or weight isn't a concern—I back the fabric with a lightweight prequilted lining. I can restitch from the wrong side, using the lining's quilting lines, which saves me a lot of time and measuring.
Bettie Russo, Battleground, WA

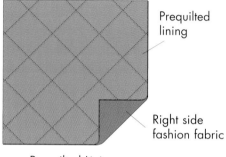

Prequilted lining

Right side fashion fabric

Prequilted Lining

Marathon Memories

My son is a marathon runner and a collector of T-shirts. I decided to do something with the pile of shirts he'd accumulated, so I made a memory quilt for his 40th birthday. I cut out the shirt fronts and backed them with fusible interfacing to stabilize them. Using muslin, I made a copy of a photo of my son crossing the finish line and used that as the center square. I made pillows from the remaining shirts, and my son now has permanent mementos of his races.
Netty Gautier, Rocky Point, NY

Another idea: Instead of simply backing T-shirt pieces with fusible interfacing, *Marlyn Foell of Satellite Beach, FL,* fuses each to muslin, which adds stability to the fabric.

Hankies Become a Quilt

A friend asked me to make a quilt using 20 antique handkerchiefs. I formed quilt blocks by stitching each handkerchief to a pastel fabric base that complemented the hankie; I joined the blocks with white sashing. Then I quilted a design in the middle of each hankie. Once I added a white border, the quilt was king-size.
Mary Jane Hofacre, Dalton, OH

Quicker Crazy Quilts

As a shortcut for sewing crazy quilt pieces, I cut a 12½" (31.8-cm) square of unprinted newsprint, pin on my crazy pieces, and zigzag them in place without turning under any hems. After I'm finished, I tear the newsprint away. I pin all the blocks before sewing, and sometimes I pin enough for four or five quilt tops at one time.

Iris Degerstrom, Cottage Grove, OR

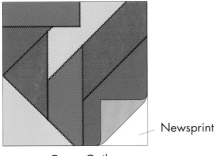

Newsprint

Crazy Quilt

Safety Pins Speed Quilting

Safety pins really speed my quilting. Rather than hand-basting the backing, the batting, and the quilt top together, I pin all the layers together with size 1 or size 2 safety pins. (I look for brass or nickel-plated pins that will not rust or corrode.) By using the small pins, I can keep my stitching lines close together without the pins interfering.

Donna Steinbach, Mitchell, SD

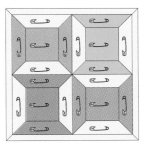

Safety Pin Basting

Get Accurate Seam Allowances

To get accurate ¼" (6-mm) seam allowances when I'm quilting, I place a lined 3" x 5" (7.6-cm x 12.7-cm) index card under the edge of the presser foot. The blue lines on the card are exactly ¼" (6 mm) apart, so I can adjust the position of my sewing machine needle using the card as a guide.

Lucy Cobb, Easley, SC

Another idea: *Marion Williams of Hazleton, PA,* found that the widest position on her sewing machine's topstitching foot is ¼" (6 mm). Using this foot to do machine quilting works simply, accurately, and quickly for her.

Templates in a Flash

I'm making a sampler quilt that has a different block design each month. Ordinarily I would make many templates, instead I take each month's pattern to a local copy center and have them make a copy onto paper that is the weight of a manila file folder. The cost is only 20 cents per copy. I cut out the cardboard and have my template in a minute or two.

Cheryl Jones, Forest Hill, MD

Another idea: *Virginia Benson of Duvall, WA,* and *Evelyn Ferguson of Everett, WA,* recycle the thick plastic sheets that come under bacon. After washing the sheets in the dishwasher to remove all the bacon residue, they cut quilting and appliqué templates from them. One side of the plastic is rough which helps prevent slipping.

Recycled Log Cabin Foundations

I save old sheets, pillowcases, and scraps of pastel fabrics traditionally used for interlining to use when I make Log Cabin quilts.

I cut out 12½" (31.8 cm) squares from these fabrics. I place a fabric scrap in the center of the square, positioned on the diagonal. Then I join additional strips to the first piece with ¼" (6-mm) seams, right sides together, in a Log Cabin design. My squares don't have to be any particular width or precisely even, but I end up with attractive, easy-to-complete blocks.

Alice Green, New Port Richey, FL

Piece a Sweatshirt

I always seems to have a ton of fleece left over when I make a sweatshirt, but it's never quite enough to make any one project. With a little creativity, I use up these bulky fleece scraps by patching the large scraps together into an interesting design. I then use my colorful patchwork fleece fabric to sew another sweatshirt as usual.

Madeline Terrell, Baton Rouge, LA

Extend Your Sewing Area

When quilting or sewing any large pieces of fabric, I set up my ironing board and adjust it to the height of my sewing machine cabinet. The ironing board provides an extended area on which to rest my project while I'm sewing.
Emmie Vance,
Polk, OH

A Thimble for Feet?

I find metal and plastic thimbles for hand-quilting to be awkward, but leather ones are too thin. After relaying this to my husband, I came home one day to find three heavy leather thimbles that he had cut from a pair of old boots. These thimbles stand up, quilt after quilt—I've only replaced them a couple of times in 10 years. It's possible to make any size and shape thimble, and the local thrift store can be a good source of used boots. Cut a strip the size you want and sew about ⅛" (3 mm) around the outside edges. The thimbles may seem stiff at first, but they soften up in no time.
Diane Rodriguez, Welches, OR

Christmas Log Cabin Wear

My daughters and I liked the effect when you sewed a Log Cabin block onto the front of a T-shirt on one of your "Sewing With Nancy" programs. I used the idea to make Christmas dresses for my four daughters.

When making the Log Cabin blocks, I reduced the width of the strips by ¼" (6 mm) for each size range. The block for my daughter who wears smaller than a size 4, for example, was made with 1¼" (3.2-cm), and the one for my daughter who wears a girl's size 12 was made with 1¾" (4.4-cm) blocks.

For each, I sewed a block to the center of a T-shirt and then added a skirt to the bottom of the shirt, using one of the fabrics from the quilt block. To make the skirt, I cut strips of fabric as long as I wanted the skirt to be (with hem and seam allowances) and twice the width of the bottom of the shirt. I gathered the fabric, stitched it to the bottom of the shirt, and hemmed the dress. I had inexpensive holiday dresses that the girls just loved!
Joni Thoman, Lockport, NY

"Quilt" a Jeans Vest

To add a decorative touch to a jeans vest for my daughter, I took a simple template used for quilting, traced the design onto the garment, and then satin-stitched over the lines using decorative thread. The result was pleasing and very easy for those of us who lack freehand talent.
Heidi McAtee, Edmond, OK

Easy Bias Piecing

Since straight piecing shows more and is bulkier than bias piecing, I like to piece my quilt borders on the bias.

Position the end of one piece of the border over the end of the second piece in an L-shape, with right sides together. Mark from corner to corner on the diagonal and sew at a 45° angle. Trim the seam. Presto! You have a perfect bias joining.

Letha Krehbiel, Moundridge, KS

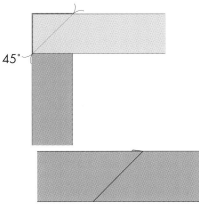

45°

Easy Bias Piecing

Ready for Cutting

I have a system that helps keep my fabrics organized (even though sometimes I have to force myself to do this, since I would rather start my project immediately). I like to use fat quarters because I can have a variety of colors and fabrics easily at hand. Fat quarters are easy to organize because I just put them in baskets according to color and then put the baskets onto the bookshelf where they are easily seen. For lengths of fabric ½ yard (.46 m) or more, I wash and press the fabric. Next, I fold the fabric in half lengthwise twice; then I hang it on a hanger.

I can choose my fabric color and lay the fabric on the cutting mat, where it is ready for rotary cutting. I can easily cut the length I need for my project. I don't have to fold the fabric at the last minute, matching selvage edges and fighting the bulk of fabric. It's always prefolded and ready to use.

Ricki Shoptaw, Longview, WA

A Dresden Plate Shortcut

When I make a Dresden Plate quilt, I seam the outer edges of each section rather than turning under the edges. This technique makes the plate so easy to appliqué and so neat looking. I'd used the technique often in finishing apron ties before I realized it could be applied to quilt making.

I meet the outer edges of each section, with right sides together, and stitch a ¼" (6-mm) seam. When I turn the pieces right side out, the edges are finished. Then I simply join the individual sections with ¼" (6-mm) seams.

Elsie Hull, Burns, OR

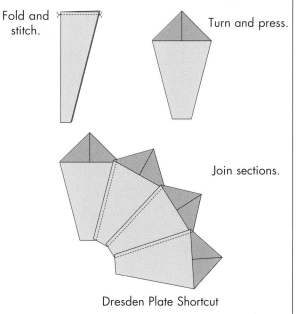

Fold and stitch.

Turn and press.

Join sections.

Dresden Plate Shortcut

Preview Seminole Patterns

I decided to include a Seminole patchwork section in one of my garments. I knew that unless I was certain what the finished patchwork would look like in the colors I chose, I could invest a lot of time and money buying different fabrics to try different patterns in several colors. Instead I bought a tablet of inexpensive craft paper in many colors, cut the desired pattern pieces (eliminating seam allowances), and taped the pieces together. In no time I previewed the finished piece. This saved me a lot of time and yardage in choosing just the right colors.

Mary Ann Sparks, Lake Wales, FL

Think Ahead

I save scraps of fabric from sewing projects for my son and daughter. Eventually I'll make each of them a crazy quilt/memory quilt. Each piece of fabric will bring back cherished memories of their childhoods.
Fannie Henline,
Wetumpka, AL

A GLOSSARY OF NOTIONS

Many "Sewing With Nancy" viewers recommend specific notions (or substitutes for specific notions) in their hints. Different viewers sometimes call the same notion by generic names: monofilament nylon thread, for example, is the same thing as transparent thread or invisible thread.

Following is a glossary of notions that are mentioned in this book. Corresponding brand names for generic products often follow the definitions. Listings for brand name items refer you to the appropriate generic product names. The list of brand names includes products available through *Nancy's Notions Catalog*. To order a copy of the catalog, see page 144. Many of these (as well as other brand name items) are available at local fabric stores.

Antitarnish fabric: A softly napped 100%-cotton fabric with a special finish to keep out gases that tarnish silver. (Kenized® Silvershield™ Silvercloth)

Bamboo Pointer & Creaser: Brand name for a tool with a pointed end for turning collars, cuffs, and lapels, and a rounded end for creasing fabric or temporarily pressing seams open.

Ban-Rol® Waistband Insert: Brand name for belting.

Basting tape: Double-sided tape that provides temporary adhesive to fabric; also available in a water-soluble version. (Wash-A-Way Basting Tape)

Beeswax: Used to strengthen thread and to reduce knotting, especially for candlewicking, quilting, and hand sewing.

Belting: Heavy interfacing material designed to stiffen belts and waistbands. (Ban-Rol® Waistband Insert)

Bodkin: A tweezerlike device used to draw elastic, ribbon, or cord through a casing. (Ezy-Pull® Bodkin)

Buttonhole cutter: A two-piece implement consisting of a flat-edge knife and a wooden block, designed for cutting open buttonholes.

Buttonhole elastic: Elastic with unknit sections at regular intervals so that an elastic waistband can be lengthened or shortened by rebuttoning a button sewn in the waistband casing. (Button-Up Elastic)

Buttonhole space tape: Tear-away tape with markings at regular intervals, used to space buttonholes evenly on a garment. (Space-Tape™)

Button-Up Elastic: Brand name for buttonhole elastic.

Clear elastic: See-through elastic noted for its ability to stretch up to three times its length without loosing elasticity.

Cording foot: A sewing machine foot with a deep channel to accommodate cords in piping, beads, or other dimensional seams. (Pearls 'N Piping™ Foot)

Disappearing Ink Marking Pen: Brand name for a temporary marker; is air soluble.

Do-Sew®: Brand name for pattern tracing material.

Double needle: Two sewing machine needles on a single shank, used with a zigzag foot to sew pintucks or to sew a double row of topstitching.

Dressmaker's carbon paper: Carbon paper especially designed for transferring markings onto fabric; several varieties of carbonless transfer paper are now available as alternatives, such as Mark•Be•Gone™ Tracing Paper and Saral Transfer Paper.

Edgestitching foot: Another generic name for a topstitching foot.

EZE-View™ Press Cloth: Brand name for a press cloth.

Ezy-Hem® Gauge: Brand name for a hem gauge.

Ezy-Pull® Bodkin: Brand name for a bodkin.

Fabric glue: A temporary or permanent adhesive used to hold fabric pieces together; some wash out, others are permanent. (Liquid Pins, Liqui Fuse™ Liquid Fusible Web™, Plexi® 400 Stretch Adhesive, Stikit Again & Again™ Glue)

Fashion Craft™ Permanent Fabric Marker: A brand name for a permanent marker; has a brush-style nib.

Fine Fuse™: Brand name for fusible web.

Fixvelours®: Brand name for hook-and-loop tape.

Flat-application elastic: Flat tape with elastic cords running through it in channels; the product is applied flat and then the cords are pulled up to achieve the desired width. (Stitch 'n Stretch™ Elastic, Stitch & Stretch™ Elastic)

Fray Check™: Brand name for seam sealant.

Fusible hem tape: A type of fusible web; comes in a narrow roll. (Stitch Witchery®)

Fusible interfacing: Nonwoven interfacing that is ironed in place; fusible on one side only; available in various weights. (Fusible Pellon®, Stacy's® Shape Flex®)

Fusible Pellon®: Brand name for fusible interfacing.

Fusible thread: Thread that can be used like common sewing thread but that bonds to fabric when ironed. (ThreadFuse™, Coats® Stitch 'n Fuse®)

Fusible web: Material that is fusible on both sides, used to bond two pieces of fabric; may be paper backed. (Wonder-Under™, Fine Fuse™, HeatnBond®, Stitch Witchery®)

Gingher® Sharpening Stone: Brand name for a sharpening stone.

Grid Grip™: Brand name for pattern tracing material; gridded paper that can be pressed and re-pressed to fabric up to 50 times; designed especially for quilting.

Hair canvas: A very stiff interfacing made of cotton, wool, or rayon with goat hair or horsehair sewn into the filling. (Pellon® Sewer's Choice)

HeatnBond®: Brand name for fusible web; is paper backed.

Hem gauge: A special ruler designed to use when marking hems at the ironing board. (Ezy-Hem® Gauge)

Hook-and-loop tape: A fastener; available in strips, squares, or dots. (Fixvelours®, Velcro®)

Horsehair: Hair of a horse's mane or tail used in hair canvas interfacing.

Invisible thread: Another generic name for transparent thread.

Jean-a-ma-jig™: Brand name for a plastic implement designed to help ease thick seams under a sewing machine needle and a presser foot.

Jiffy Grip™: Brand name for nonskid fabric.

Kenized® Silvershield™ Silvercloth: Brand name for an antitarnish fabric.

Lingerie/bobbin thread: Braided, stretchy thread that is ideal for machine embroidery and for sewing lingerie.

Liquid Fusible Web: Part of the brand name for a fabric glue; see also Liqui Fuse™ Liquid Fusible Web™.

Liquid Pins: Brand name for fabric glue; washes away.

Liquid stabilizer: A wash-away product that, when dry, stabilizes fabric for buttonholes, appliqué, and other techniques. (Perfect Sew)

Liqui Fuse™ Liquid Fusible Web™: Brand name for fabric glue; can be washed out before being ironed (once ironed, it becomes permanent).

Little Foot™: Brand name for a transparent presser foot notched at ¼" before and after the needle position; especially useful when quilting.

Loop shade tape: Tape with fabric loops or plastic rings used to make balloon, cloud, and Roman shades; a variety of curtain and drapery tapes are also available, including French pleating tape, shirring tape, smocking tape, and box pleat folding tape.

Mark•Be•Gone™ Marking Pen: Brand name for a temporary marker; is water soluble.

Metroflock Woolly Stretch Nylon: Brand name for woolly nylon thread.

Monofilament nylon thread: Another generic name for transparent thread.

Naugahyde™: Brand name for vinyl-coated fabric; marine-quality Naugahyde is strong enough to withstand use in boats and other wet settings.

Needle Grabbers: Brand name for rubber grips that help pull needles through heavy fabric.

No-Fray: Brand name for seam sealant.

Nonroll elastic: Elastic available in up to 2" widths (5.1 cm) that is designed to lie flat and to resist the tendency to roll or to buckle. (No-Roll Elastic)

Nonskid fabric: Fabric used on the bottoms of pajama feet and for other applications. (Jiffy Grip™, SafeTred)

Overcast guide foot: A foot for zigzag sewing machines that provides a guide for maintaining even stitches at the edge of a piece of fabric. (Satinedge™ Foot)

Pattern-Sta™: Brand name for spray adhesive.

Pattern tracing material: A paper or synthetic material especially designed for use in copying patterns; particularly helpful when using multisize patterns. (Do-Sew®, Grid Grip™)

Pearl Crown Rayon Thread: Brand name for rayon thread.

Pearls 'N Piping™ Foot: Brand name for a cording foot.

Pellon® Sewer's Choice: Brand name for hair canvas.

Pen Touch Pen: Brand name for a permanent marker.

Perfect Sew: Brand name for a liquid stabilizer.

Permanent marker: A pen or a pencil whose mark will withstand laundering; those designed especially for fabric won't feather or bleed when applied or smear when dry. (Fashion Craft™ Permanent Fabric Marker, Pen Touch Pen, Pigma Micron Permanent Pen)

Pigma Micron Permanent Pen: Brand name for a permanent marker.

Pintuck foot: A sewing machine foot grooved with five, seven, or nine channels; previously sewn rows of pin tucking fit in the channels, allowing even stitching.

Plexi® 400 Stretch Adhesive: Brand name for a fabric glue; permanent but retains its flexibility.

Press cloth: Material placed over an item while pressing to protect the fabric finish. (EZE-View™, Steam 'n Shape™)

Quilter's Clean Erase™ Marking Pencil: Brand name for temporary marker; is erasable.

Quilter's Deluxe Ruler Handle: Brand name for a quilter's tool handle.

Quilter's ruler: A precision-cut acrylic ruler designed for use with a rotary cutter and a mat; may have special lines to make cutting fabric at angles easier.

Quilter's tool handle: A plastic handle with suction cups to attach it to an acrylic quilter's ruler (or other surface). (Quilter's Deluxe Ruler Handle)

Rayon thread: A colorful, high-luster thread used for machine embroidery and other decorative applications. (Pearl Crown Rayon Thread, Sulky® Embroidery Thread)

Ribbon Floss™: A decorative, braided, 1/16"-wide (1.5-mm) rayon ribbon.

Rotary cutter and mat: The tools that revolutionized quilting; a rotary cutter has a circular blade mounted in an easy-grip handle; the special companion cutting mat has a textured, nonskid surface and a gridded pattern for cutting accurate straight lines and angles.

SafeTred: Brand name for nonskid fabric.

Satinedge™ Foot: Brand of overcast guide foot; has an adjustable width guide.

Seam sealant: A liquid that reinforces buttonholes, stops fraying on cut edges, and secures threads at ends of seams. (Fray Check™, No-Fray)

Seams Great®: Brand name for a sheer seam finish.

Seam stabilizing tape: Tape added at the shoulders, a neckline, and gathers to help seams keep their shape. (Stay-Tape™)

Serger reference cards: 3" x 5" (7.6-cm x 12.7-cm) index cards that are preprinted to record serger settings used for specific fabric types, including stitch type, needles, and stitch length.

Sewer's Fix-it Tape: Brand name for a soft, see-through adhesive-backed sewing tape.

Sew Through Sports Elastic: Brand name for sport elastic.

Sharpening stone: A whetstone especially designed for sharpening scissors. (Gingher® Sharpening Stone)

Sheer seam finish: A clear product used to cover and protect raw edges without adding bulk. (Seams Great®)

Sleeve board: An ironing board accessory that is shaped especially for use when pressing sleeves; other accessories include a ham (to press curved shapes such as darts, sleeve caps, and curved seams), a seam roll (to press long seams without seam edge impressions), and a clapper (to flatten collars, pleats, facings, and other bulky details).

Space-Tape™: Brand name for buttonhole space tape.

Sport elastic: A wide elastic with four unbraided rows within the elastic that serve as sewing channels; some brands use blue sewing channels, others use white or other colors. (Sew Through Sports Elastic)

Spray adhesive: Used to temporarily secure patterns to fabric without pins or to hold together seam allowances in slippery fabrics such as satin. (Pattern-Sta™)

Stacy's® Shape Flex: Brand name for fusible interfacing.

Stay-Tape™: Brand name for seam stabilizing tape.

Steam 'n Shape™: Brand name for a press cloth.

Stikit Again & Again Glue™: Brand name for fabric glue; pressure-sensitive and permanent.

Stitch 'n Fuse®: Brand name for fusible thread.

Stitch 'n Stretch™ Elastic: Brand name for flat-application elastic.

Stitch & Stretch™ Elastic: Brand name for flat-application elastic.

Stitch Witchery®: Brand name for fusible web; sold in strips and rolls.

Stitch-N-Tear®: Brand name for tear-away stabilizer.

Sulky® Embroidery Thread: Brand name for rayon thread.

Synthetic suede: Woven fabric that simulates the look and the feel of suede. (Ultrasuede®)

Tailor's chalk: Makes removable, crisp, accurate lines on sewing projects.

Tear-away stabilizer: Lightweight, nonwoven stabilizer that can be sewn through and then torn away. (Stitch-N-Tear®, Totally Stable)

Teflon presser foot: A presser foot with a Teflon® coating on the underside to make vinyl fabrics glide under the presser foot.

Temporary marker: A pen or a pencil that can be used to mark fabric, and the marks can later be removed or will disappear; includes air-soluble (disappears within 24 hours without washing), water-soluble (requires a drop of cold water to remove), and erasable. (Disappearing Ink Marking Pen, Mark•Be•Gone Marking Pen, Quilter's Clean Erase™ Marking Pencil, Ultimate Marking Pencil, Wash-Out Pencil, Wonder Marker)

ThreadFuse™: Brand name for fusible thread.

Topstitching foot: A sewing machine foot with an adjustable guide to keep fabric edges at a correct distance from the needle; also called an edgestitching foot.

Totally Stable: A tear-away stabilizer; irons on.

Transparent thread: Nylon monofilament thread, available in clear or smoke; also called invisible thread. (Wonder Thread)

Ultimate Marking Pencil: Brand name for a temporary marker; is water soluble.

Ultrasuede®: Brand name for synthetic suede.

Velcro®: Brand name for hook-and-loop tape.

Vinyl-coated fabric: Woven fabric coated with vinyl to make it water resistant. (Naugahyde™)

Wash-Away Plastic Stabilizer: Brand name for a water-soluble stabilizer.

Wash-A-Way Basting Tape: Brand name for basting tape; is water soluble.

Wash-Out Pencil: Brand name for a temporary marker; is water soluble.

Water soluble stabilizer: A plastic stabilizer that washes away. (Perfect Sew, Wash-Away Plastic Stabilizer)

Wonder Marker: Brand name for a temporary marker; is water soluble.

Wonder Thread: Brand name for transparent thread.

Wonder-Under®: Brand name for fusible web; is paper backed.

Woolly Lock: Brand name for woolly nylon thread.

Woolly nylon thread: A superstretchy, texturized nylon thread used for soft, comfortable seams. (Metroflock Woolly Stretch Nylon, Woolly Lock)

INDEX

Nancy Zieman—businesswoman, home economist, and national sewing authority—is the producer and hostess of the popular show "Sewing With Nancy," which appears exclusively on public television stations. The show, broadcast since September 1982, is the longest-airing sewing program on television. Nancy organizes each show in a how-to format, concentrating on step-by-step instructions.

Nancy also produces and hosts *Sewing With Nancy* videos. Each video contains three segments from her television program. Currently, there are 28 one-hour videos available to retailers, educators, libraries, and sewing groups.

In addition, Nancy is founder and president of Nancy's Notions, which publishes *Nancy's*

Notions Sewing Catalog. This large catalog contains more than 4,000 products, including sewing books, notions, videos, and fabrics.

Nancy has written several books including: *10-20-30 Minutes to Sew, The Best of Sewing With Nancy,* and *Sewing Express*. In each book, Nancy emphasizes efficient sewing techniques that produce professional results.

Nancy was named the 1988 Entrepreneurial Woman of the Year by the Wisconsin Women Entrepreneurs Association. In 1991, she also received the National 4-H Alumni Award. She is a member of the American Home Economics Association and the American Home Sewing & Craft Association.

Nancy lives in Beaver Dam, Wisconsin, with her husband/business partner, Rich, and their two sons, Ted and Tom.

For a complete line of sewing notions, turn to...

Nancy's Notions Sewing Catalog

- Nancy Zieman's catalog for sewing, serging, and quilting enthusiasts.
- More than 4,000 products, including books, notions, videos, fabrics, and supplies!
- Value prices with built-in discounts!
- 100% satisfaction guaranteed!

For your free *Nancy's Notions Sewing Catalog*, send your name and address to:

Nancy's Notions
P.O. Box 683
Dept. 2316
Beaver Dam, Wisconsin 53916

Or call 1-800-833-0690.